UNION J

UNION J

THE UNAUTHORISED BIOGRAPHY

REBECCA GREY

HarperCollins*Publishers*

HarperCollins*Publishers*
77–85 Fulham Palace Road,
Hammersmith, London W6 8JB

www.harpercollins.co.uk

First published by HarperCollins*Publishers* 2013

1 3 5 7 9 10 8 6 4 2

A catalogue record of this book is
available from the British Library

HB ISBN 978-0-00-752949-0
EB ISBN 978-0-00-752951-3

Printed and bound in Great Britain by
Clays Ltd, St Ives plc

MIX
Paper from
responsible sources
FSC **FSC C007454**
www.fsc.org

CONTENTS

ON TOP OF THE WORLD

Shards of light pierced the ceiling as four plinths rose slowly from the stage. The atmosphere inside Manchester Arena on 27 January 2013 was electric as the 23,000-strong crowd began cheering and hollering. This was the moment they'd been waiting for and the anticipation was at fever pitch. Slowly, the plinths rose up many feet into the air, in front of a dramatic starlit backdrop, and the thousands of fans in the audience began shouting and crying even louder. The spotlights shone down onto the four boys each standing on a plinth as they stopped, positioning the singers high above the arena crowd, desperate to hear from them, many feet below. Illuminated by the dramatic light effects and with adrenalin coursing through their bodies, each boy took his microphone and began singing the first few bars of Leona Lewis's huge hit, 'Bleeding Love'. It was a moment none of them could have imagined happening to them just a few months ago when their dreams were just that – dreams.

On the far left, wearing a blazer and trousers like the rest of the group, with his hair styled into a sharp quiff, was Jamie 'JJ' Hamblett, 24 at that moment. A genuinely decent guy, with handsome looks and a past career as a jockey, he had thought his future lay on the racetracks of Britain, not in its arenas. Standing next to him was Josh Cuthbert, only 20, but already a veteran of previous boybands that hadn't worked out. Devastatingly handsome, charming and with a self-deprecating, emotional side, Josh was finally enjoying his moment in the sun as a born pop singer and heartthrob. Next alongside him was Jaymi Hensley, the boy with the heartbreakingly amazing voice. His talent for performing had been evident since his childhood in Luton, but the 23-year-old had been disappointed time and time again trying to get his career off the ground. Now every inch the star, with his tousled hair, bags of charisma and magnetic personality, he poured every inch of his emotion into the performance. As the song moved on, George Shelley, the youngest member of the group at just 19, took the second verse as a solo. With his sideswept brown curls and incredible cheekbones, he had the pop idol looks and sweet personality that made all around him melt.

The plinths began slowly descending back down as the song turned into 'Broken Strings' by James Morrison and Nelly Furtado. As it built to a crescendo, the four boys began harmonising effortlessly together and stepped onto the stage, walking around and acknowledging the fans, who screamed with delight as their idols noticed them. The spotlights shone red, yellow and blue over the band and dry ice billowed around, highlighting their similarities and differences at the same time. They were a group, dressed with clothes and hair-styles that echoed each other, but they were also individuals, moving separately around the stage, each of them letting their distinctive voices shine. 'One more time, please sing with us, Manchester!' called Josh, as the song reached its climax. Fireworks poured down around them onto the stage as the fans in the audience launched into the loudest screams and claps yet. Jaymi and Josh walked to the front section of the stage, which jutted out into the audience. 'How are we feeling, Manchester?' yelled Jaymi, as he took in the amazing sight before him, pointing at the thousands of people who cheered his every word. The reception was even more fevered when George, stage right, began speaking. 'You're all having a good night, yeah?' he asked, as he waved at the fans hanging onto his every word and movement. 'We just want to say a massive, massive thank you to each and every one of you for the support you've given us over the last few months,' Jaymi told the audience. Behind him, George punched the air in delight and did a little star jump. Just like the other boys onstage, he was filled with happiness at this amazing moment.

They were Union J, and this was The X Factor 2013 Live Tour. The band hadn't existed until only a few months previously, and it had been a journey of laughter and tears, highs and lows that had pushed them all to the limits of joy and sorrow. It might have been early days for the group, but thanks to their involvement in the biggest TV show in Britain, they were already stars. With their debut single about to come out that summer, and the group set to become one of the UK's biggest boybands, Union J's future was golden. But getting there had been far from easy …

CHAPTER I
ALL ABOUT THE BOYS

Jaymi

The beginning of the 1990s was an exciting time in Britain, as people waved goodbye to the Eighties and ushered in a brand-new decade, with new fashions and new music on the horizon. And on 24 February 1990, just a couple of days before dramatic storms hit the country, a little baby was born whose love of music and performing would change his life – Jaymi Hensley. Born James William Hensley in Luton, a town a little over 30 miles north of London, Jaymi was the first child for his mum Jackie and dad David (if he'd been a girl, he would have been called Amber!).

They lived in the village of Stopsley, where Jaymi's mum worked in the local newsagent's, Hendersons. Jaymi was a cute little boy, and right from an early age had a close relationship with his mother – his first word, in fact, was 'Mum'. He always had lots of respect and love for Jackie, who he called his 'hero'. Many years later, when he was in Union J, Jaymi would tell *Cosmopolitan* magazine: 'We've all been brought up by strong, independent women. We're all mummy's boys!' He started at the local school, Putteridge Infant and Junior School, in September 1994, proudly wearing his dark-blue uniform as he stepped through the school gates for the first time. As well as starting school, there was another big change happening to Jaymi back then, as his little brother Aaron arrived the same year.

From a young age, it was clear that Jaymi had a strong vocal talent and a flair for dramatics. In her spare time, Jaymi's mum Jackie was a dance teacher and choreographer for local amateur dramatics group The Phoenix Players, and it wasn't long before Jaymi wanted to join her. He took to the stage like a duck to water and the first musical he appeared in was *Bye Bye Birdie*. As Jaymi grew up he also started to form his own taste in music – developing a fondness for female singers with incredible voices. The first single he bought, aged nine, was Christina Aguilera's 'Genie in a Bottle', a huge pop-dance track that was all over the radio during the summer of 1999, and soon Jaymi also got into Beyoncé. It fast became evident that Jaymi himself had a sensational voice, and as well as singing regularly, he began taking ballet lessons, too.

Aged 11, Jaymi moved up into Putteridge High School, and his love for performing grew even stronger. Despite having lots of schoolwork, he managed to fit in starring in the Phoenix Players' production of *Blitz!*, a musical by Lionel Bart, who also wrote *Oliver!* But his cheeky, rebellious side sometimes saw him get into trouble at school. Together with his friend Stacey, Jaymi once hid every single clock in the school – a joke that spiralled out of control when the two pranksters got found out and suspended. And it wasn't the first time Jaymi was suspended – the next time was for having a streak in his hair, and the time after that for wearing an earring. Jaymi was determined not to be just like all those around him, and instead to be himself. 'Be honest and forge your own path in life' is still his personal motto.

During his teen years, Jaymi poured all his energy into pursuing his dreams of a career in performance. He realised that he had a special talent and felt most alive when he was onstage. So with the support of his friends and family, he started attending weekend classes at the prestigious Sylvia Young Theatre School in London, where lots of the students had gone on to become famous and successful. Spice Girl Emma Bunton, pop star Rita Ora, late singer Amy Winehouse and actresses Kara Tointon and Denise Van Outen had all gone there and went on to achieve amazing things, so Jaymi knew it was one of the best places to learn his craft. And a short while later he met a friend at Sylvia Young who would become very important in his life in the future – a good-looking younger boy called Joshua Cuthbert.

As well as spending all his spare time singing and dancing, Jaymi also got into the *Twilight* books. As a sensitive Pisces, he adored the dramatic romance of the series and loved them even more when they were turned into the films starring Robert Pattinson and Kristen Stewart. 'I love *Twilight*; I'm a bit of a softy. I'm a proper RPattz fan,' he said. No wonder that a highlight of his time on *The X Factor* was attending the *Breaking Dawn – Part 2* London premiere.

After leaving school Jaymi decided to try and go for a career in pop music – and originally it seemed that his dreams would come true more quickly than he could have imagined. Aged 16, he tried out for a new boyband and was thrilled when he was accepted as one of Code5. Alongside bandmates Mitch Carroll, Dean Stansby, Joss Wilson and

Chris Johnson, Jaymi threw his all into the new group. As the youngest member of the band, he found himself performing at huge arenas up and down the country, when Code5 landed a supporting-act slot on Westlife's The Love Tour. He got a huge thrill from singing in front of such big crowds, and hoped that one day Code5 would get to be as big as the Irish supergroup, managed by Jaymi's future *X Factor* mentor, Louis Walsh. 'I can't stop smiling. It was amazing. People keep taking pictures of me and saying well done in the street, it's like star treatment,' he told the local newspaper, *Luton Today*. 'You imagine in your head how the other half live, but it's all above your imagination.'

Things were going well: following the live tour, Code5 headed into the recording studio to lay down some tracks; they recorded a mixture of new songs and old classics, such as Lionel Richie's 'Hello'. But despite this positive start, Code5 didn't find any real success, and soon a disappointed Jaymi decided to go solo. He began singing at lots of the Gay Pride events, and loved the buzz he got from being in front of an audience – even writing on his Myspace page how he feels 'happiest when performing live'. As a solo artist, Jaymi thought he'd found his big break again – winning a talent contest and being signed by Dance Crazy management. He began work on his debut single – a cover of a Nick Kamen hit from the 1980s – but yet again he found that success eluded him. Things were proving a struggle, and to make ends meet he had to find part-time work as a singing and dancing teacher. He kept plugging away at his dream, though, and at the end of 2010 entered the Open Mic UK competition. There, he dazzled the judges with a rendition of Leona

Lewis's 'Bleeding Love', but missed out on the winner's trophy, coming fourth in his age category. It was another near-miss for Jaymi, who was finding that reaching the top in showbiz was tough. But he didn't let his dreams die, and all the time he had the support of his friends and family – especially mum Jackie, who always knew he would end up doing what he loved for a living. 'If Jaymi wasn't a singer, I don't know what else he could be, really – as he's not much good at anything else!' she joked to *The X Factor*, years later.

But despite all the disappointments so far in Jaymi's career, he was determined not to give up. He knew that fame and success weren't going to be handed to him on a plate, and he would have to keep plugging away at every opportunity he could grab. A big fan of *The X Factor*, he knew that getting seen on screen could be the big break he'd been waiting for. So, by 2011, Jaymi was ready for another crack at fame. He'd joined a new boyband with some friends from Luton. They called themselves Brooklyn after pointing at an atlas with their eyes closed and landing on the city of New York! Having only recently formed the band, within a few months they were travelling to Cardiff to audition for *The X Factor*. Performing in front of judges Gary Barlow, Tulisa Contostavlos, Kelly Rowland and Louis Walsh, they impressed with their version of Cee Lo Green's 'Forget You'. Gary wanted to hear more, so the boys sang Jason Derulo's 'In My Head' – causing a divide between the judges. They got through the audition stage after Jaymi vowed to Gary that they'd work hard. Determination was etched all over his face. But yet again his dreams were dashed when the group was kicked out at Bootcamp stage. Things were hard for Jaymi;

instead of making a living doing what he loved, he had to earn money doing what he described as 'rubbish' jobs, such as working in a call centre. But the absolute worst job for Jaymi was packing items for online retailer Amazon. Standing by a conveyor belt wasn't the stuff of his dreams, so he kept plugging away at his singing career.

He'd had so many false starts in music that Jaymi wondered if he would ever make the big time. But after getting noticed as part of Brooklyn, pop manager Julian White thought he had what it takes. He put together a new boyband called Rewind, which included Jaymi's friend Josh Cuthbert from Sylvia Young and three other boys, one of whom was a former jockey called 'JJ' Hamblett.

JJ

You would hardly expect to find a future pop star on the racecourses of Britain. Set in beautiful countryside, the town of Newmarket is where horseracing was born hundreds of years ago and it still dominates the life of everyone who lives there, claiming 'horseracing is breathed on every corner'. It couldn't be more different from the bright, bustling lights of London and the world of music and show-biz. But, on 25 May 1988, James Paul Hamblett was born in the Suffolk town, and for most of his life horses were his focus. He didn't ever expect to end up as a pop star – he was going to be a jockey!

He came from a horsey family: JJ's dad, Paul, had been a jockey and so had his uncle, Martin, who trained horses in Germany, and a distant cousin – Liam Heard – was a jockey, too. JJ's older brother Ashley had been born just a year before him, and the two boys grew up incredibly close to each other. So close that often their mum, Karin, worried about them! 'JJ and his brother had a secret language with each other – they sounded like the Clangers!' she recalled. 'I was so worried I had to take them to the speech therapist.' From a young age, JJ and Ashley were riding ponies every weekend, and JJ – quieter than confident Ashley – wanted to do everything his big brother did.

Despite being horse-crazy, JJ still got into his music. The first single he ever bought, aged 10, was 'I Want It That Way' and he soon became a huge Backstreet Boys' fan. He also developed a big crush on sexy *Baywatch* star Pamela Anderson! But with his two obsessions of horses and music, JJ didn't leave much room for concentrating in class at Soham Village College and Scaltback Middle School and he often found himself getting into trouble with teachers. A big chatterbox, JJ found that teachers got annoyed at his constant talking. It frustrated his cooking teacher so much that she even threw a pencil at his head once!

Animals were a big part of JJ's life. His family owned a stunning German pointer dog, but he went through a traumatic experience with this dog when he was just 11. Told he was able to take the dog for a walk, JJ proudly set off, determined not to disobey his dad's instructions to keep the dog on the lead at all times. But he forgot and took the lead off near a local motorway – whereupon the dog ran into the traffic and was hit by a car. Poor JJ ran home in terror and the RSPCA ended up bringing the dog back. He never forgot the experience.

After leaving school at 16, JJ threw himself into the horse world full time and started working for trainers in Newmarket. His dream had always been to work for Sir Michael Stoute, a 10-time champion trainer, but his dad, Paul, hadn't been sure he would get the opportunity. 'Dad asked me who I wanted to work for. I said Sir Michael Stoute, but he thought that, with me being only 14 [at the time], he wouldn't want to take me on,' he said in an interview as a young rider. JJ was over the moon when he eventually became Sir Michael's apprentice at just 16 years old. The experienced trainer became a valued mentor to JJ – just like Louis Walsh would be on *The X Factor* – offering him advice and tips on how to improve. 'Even when I have an outside ride, he'll watch the race and have a word with me afterwards, telling me what I did right and what I did wrong. It's a great help,' he said at the time.

JJ worked for Sir Michael for four years while he began jockeying professionally. It was hard work, but he loved it, and he was proud of his older brother Ashley, who was apprenticed to trainer Luca Cumani. The boys spent their lives criss-crossing the country competing in races, trying to build up experience and a number of winners on the racecourse. In spare moments JJ and Ashley would sit on the sofa at home, watching their rides back on video to see where they might have improved. Dad Paul was always behind them, encouraging them to race as much as they could. 'He keeps asking, "Why haven't you got a ride today? Phone your agent and ask why you don't have a ride,"' said JJ at the time. 'Then he tells us to go for a run or something, to get us out of the house.' While a horse-mad teenager, JJ's little sister Otea was born, and he dotes on her to this day.

During this time, JJ even rode one of Her Majesty the Queen's horses and was then lucky enough to meet Her Majesty. 'Once or twice a year, she would pop into the yard to check on her horses – it was so weird seeing her,' he told the *Daily Express*. 'She sauntered in wearing Wellington boots as if it was normal – and she walked into the horses' box that I was in at the time. She said hello, fed the horses grass and left. Apart from *The X Factor*, it was the most surreal moment of my life.' Living and breathing flat racing, Ashley and JJ's bond grew ever stronger, and they were each other's biggest fans. 'When I ride against Ashley, if I can't win, I want him to win instead,' said JJ.

But a career in horseracing wasn't to be. JJ was just 21 when he realised that he would have to give up his racing dreams. As a flat jockey, it was important he kept his weight at a very low level: if the jockey was too heavy, it would slow down the horse. At a regular weight of just 7st 12lb, he was much lighter than other guys his own age and ate a special diet at home to keep him at the right frame. At 18, JJ had no problems in keeping his weight down, saying, 'I don't have to watch what I eat, but I don't eat that much anyway – I hate getting full up.' But as he grew older, it became a struggle. He reluctantly realised he would have to quit the saddle and find something else to focus on in his life. It was a huge decision for JJ to take – horses were his family's world. Still, he could be proud of his successes – by the time he stopped competing in October 2009 he'd ridden in over 260 race rides and had 24 wins in just four years of appearing on the racecourse. He wasn't ready to give up horses for good, though, and carried on as a part-time work-rider for Newmarket trainer John Gosden, taking his horse out every morning.

JJ decided to take this opportunity to try to make it in singing, acting and modelling – something he'd always secretly dreamed of. 'I have always loved singing but never had the bottle,' he told the *Newmarket Journal*. 'When I stopped race riding it gave me the drive to do something else.' With his chiselled good looks and toned body he signed up to a modelling agency and began attending auditions to try to land acting parts. One of his first was for a BBC series called *The Cut*. Although he didn't get the role, JJ's experience was growing and he was really enjoying this new challenge in his life. With the same drive and focus he'd previously applied to horseriding, he was determined to make it in the world of acting, but things were proving difficult. By 22, he'd been involved with a couple of failed singing projects and done a bit of acting but, as he himself admitted, 'nothing really took off'.

But one day in 2011, JJ was contacted out of the blue by a songwriter who'd seen his picture on his agency website. US-based songwriter Kasey Monroe had seen something in JJ's publicity shots and got in touch with him, asking if he could sing. JJ recorded a clip of his singing voice on YouTube, which impressed Kasey, who'd worked with some of the biggest names in pop, including Madonna and Westlife. She put JJ in touch with Julian White, a music manager who was putting together a new boyband. He was working with two ex-members of a band called Brooklyn who'd appeared on *The X Factor* earlier that year – and one of them happened to be a certain Jaymi Hensley! The boys hit it off straight away and JJ was hopeful that this would be the big break he'd been waiting for. 'This is a fantastic chance for me and I'm really excited,' he told the local paper in Newmarket. At the time, JJ was known as Jamie, but he quickly realised that with another member also called Jaymi, although it was spelled differently, it wouldn't work. He came up with a new nickname for himself – JJ, standing for 'Jockey Jamie'! Having met up with Jaymi and Josh, JJ was onto something good, and the next year would change his life forever.

Josh

In the middle of the summer of 1992, Britain was gripped by Olympic fever. The whole country cheered on Linford Christie as he won the Men's 100m in Barcelona, but in the village of Winkfield, near Ascot in Berkshire, Kathryn and Graeme Cuthbert had something more important to focus on. They'd just had their first baby, Joshua Thomas John Cuthbert, who'd been born on 28 July. With his big sparkling blue eyes, he was a gorgeous boy from day one, and as he grew up he loved nothing more than playing with his favourite toy, Olly the Octopus, and kicking a football about in the garden. He started at the local Cranbourne Primary School at age four, and aged seven he was chuffed to bits when his little brother Callum was born, followed three years later by his sister Victoria.

It was a normal, happy childhood, filled with school and football practice. Josh supported Chelsea and was already showing a strong talent for the game himself. He got into pop music, buying 'Don't Stop Movin' by S Club 7 as his first ever single, and enjoyed playing the class clown. Despite his cheeky side, Josh was a softy, too, always looking after animals. Throughout his childhood he had a hamster and a goldfish and loved nothing better than going to the zoo. Even now, he adores his cat Oreo, who he calls the 'mascot' of Union J! But as a child, no one in his family knew of his secret skill – singing. That was until one day when, aged 10, he landed the role of Scrooge in his school's production of *A Christmas Carol*. 'I had no idea he had a voice – we were blown away by him singing,' Josh's mum Kathryn told the local paper. 'We got him straight into Stagecoach in Bracknell, who told him to audition for *Chitty Chitty Bang Bang*.' Within a few months, young Josh's life was transformed. At just 11, he landed the role of George in the West End production of *Chitty Chitty Bang Bang*. It was an incredible experience for a young boy – appearing at the historic London Palladium for nine months alongside stars like Christopher Biggins and the late star Stephen Gately, whose previous band Boyzone had been managed by Louis Walsh. His family were thrilled – especially his nan Jean, who spent over £800 on tickets, going to see her grandson in the show every week!

Although he'd already had an amazing break in acting early on in his life, Josh still lived a regular life, moving up to Charters School in Sunningdale when he was 11. With his good looks, he began getting lots of attention from girls, but his heart was reserved for someone else – his PE teacher! He developed a huge crush on the gorgeous hockey player, whose beauty hadn't escaped the other boys in his school – Josh confessed that most of them tried to get a look at her when she was playing a match. As he grew up, Josh's romantic side emerged and he had his first kiss aged 15, playing Spin the Bottle. At school, he was a real character who left an impression on all those around him. 'He brought a smile to the face, could be a bit cheeky, but had a sparkle about him,' said headteacher Martyn Parker.

After that taste of the big time with *Chitty Chitty Bang Bang*, Josh began to think seriously about making singing his aim in life. His other passion had been football, and he'd played for quite a few teams, including Ascot Juniors, but an injury put paid to his sporting dreams. So instead he focused on singing and in early 2007 he asked his mum and dad if he could audition for that year's *X Factor*. Leona Lewis had won the year before and it would be Josh's first opportunity to audition for the top-rated show, as that year was the first they'd lowered the minimum age for participants from 16 to 14. Having turned 14 the summer before, Josh just squeaked in and his mum Kathryn reluctantly agreed to let him go. It was an amazing eye-opener for Josh, who reached the Bootcamp stage before being turned down. 'I was his chaperone and it was a very intense experience,' said Josh's mum. 'He was probably too young then.' While at *The X Factor* he also met Blair Dreelan, a singer who was auditioning as part of his band 4th Ba5e. They hit it off, and when 4th Ba5e split up, Josh and Blair started a group together called M4. Although that didn't work out either, they stayed good friends and Blair was to play a key role in Josh's future.

After his GCSEs, Josh went to Farnborough Sixth Form College, although he still hadn't given up on his dream of making it in the music industry. Having attended the Sylvia Young Theatre School's Saturday classes regularly for a few years, he'd made friends with Jaymi Hensley, another talented singer a couple of years older than himself. Together they talked about their passion for making it in music and before long Josh thought his big moment had come. Aged just 17, he won a place in a boyband called Replay and they signed a two-year management contract. He hoped that this meant his pop dreams were about to come true, although progress with Replay was slow and he wasn't sure they were going to be successful. But soon another incredible opportunity came up that would rock Josh's world. 'About a year into the contract, I got approached by Jayne Collins, who was The Wanted's manager,' Josh explained. 'She'd seen me performing with Replay and wanted me to join The Wanted as the fifth member.' Josh met up with Max and the rest of the Wanted boys and their management where they outlined plans for the band. It sounded amazing and Josh desperately wanted to leave his current group and join The Wanted, but it proved impossible. 'Me and my parents spent a lot of money trying to get me out of the contract, but there was nothing we could do – I was tied down,' he said. 'I missed out on a massive opportunity there. Every time I hear them I kick myself.'

Josh was gutted. He thought he'd missed his big break – after all, how many opportunities to join a successful boyband would occur in his life? But he was determined not to give up, to think positively and keep going. He carried on auditioning when he could, fitting it in around his studies until he left college in 2010. Josh took on jobs to make ends meet, including one stint selling mobile phones and then another working in an office doing IT sales. Although he found the work 'really boring', he had no other options until fame came calling again. But there were no guarantees. In his lowest moments Josh couldn't help but wonder whether he would ever be able to sing for a living. His next big adventure came when he joined another boyband, this time called The Boulevard. Alongside bandmates Ryan Davies, Andy Rice and Alistar Jay, they supported Boyzone in a series of gigs across Ireland. Yet again, it was a near-miss for Josh, as the band had hoped to sign a record deal, but none materialised. It was a difficult time for Josh, especially because in 2011 his beloved nan died, leaving him gutted. 'She struggled as a single mum to raise a family and we had nothing,' he said. 'She could always sing, and I grew up listening to her sing to us as kids. She always taught me to be humble and take every chance you get, as things happen for a reason.'

And things were definitely about to happen for Josh – finally. Now well known among music managers thanks to his stints in various bands, his stunning model looks and voice, he was snapped up with his friend Jaymi to join another new band called Rewind. There were five of them in total, with Billy Ashley, Ben Weedon and an ex-jockey called JJ Hamblett rounding out the group. Rewind started gigging around the country at various Pride events, but the boys weren't happy with how things were going. Three of them – Josh, JJ and Jaymi – decided to change managers and go with Blair Dreelan instead, who had by then moved into music management. (He'd also had a brush with tabloid notoriety himself when his girlfriend, Sarah Robinson, left him for *The X Factor*'s 2010 winner, Matt Cardle!) It had been a whirlwind few months, but the buzz between the three guys was there – and after the rollercoaster journey they'd all been on in their earlier attempts at a pop career, they all hoped that this would be the band that stuck. And as a newly formed three-piece, they needed a new name. With all their initials the same, it seemed like destiny: Triple J were born.

George

George Shelley grew up surrounded by music. He was born in Bristol on 27 July 1993 – just one day less than a year after Josh! – and his nurse mum Toni decided to name her third son after one of the patients she'd bonded with. Even as a toddler, he couldn't wait to start playing musical instruments and began singing as soon as he could talk. His mum would fill up bottles with uncooked rice so little George could turn them into maracas, and an early photo shows him as a cute toddler, with baby-blond hair and dimples, sitting proudly behind his Mickey Mouse drumkit. 'George, even as a young boy, always wanted to join in and used to pretend he was playing on the drums, using a saucepan and a wooden spoon,' Toni told the *Bristol Post* newspaper. 'He has always been the sort of person who could pick up an instrument and play it – a talent he got from his granddad.' George's granddad, Dave, a retired policeman, was a real rock'n'roller, playing in many bands – he was to play an influential role in his grandson's life.

George was born into a big family: he has two older brothers, Tom – who is his half-brother – and William. When George was nearly three, his little sister Harriet arrived. 'I remember walking past my mum and dad's room,' he told *Bliss* magazine. 'My mum told me to put my head on her belly and she said, "That's your sister."' Sadly, after Harriet was born, George's mum Toni and his dad Dominic split up. George stayed with his mum, living in a 'really small house' in Clevedon and going to Happy Hours Day Nursery. He then started at Backwell Infant School, moving on to Golden Valley Primary School and then Yeo Moor Junior School as his family moved house a lot. George was a smiley, sweet little boy and began showing an enthusiasm for the guitar, which his mum Toni also played, often performing at pubs, clubs and festivals with songs she'd written herself. The family wanted to encourage George to explore his musical talent, but they couldn't afford to pay for lessons. So with some help from his granddad Dave, George began teaching himself to play guitar and was so excited when he got his own guitar for his 13th birthday. He spent hours honing his skills, practising chords and trying to learn his favourite pop songs, especially those by the Black Eyed Peas. 'Where Is the Love?' was one of his top tunes.

But George also had to deal with some difficult times, too. His brother Will, who had joined the Royal Marines, went off for his first tour of duty in Afghanistan when his little brother was only 13. George had to deal with the fact that Will was risking his life for his country, and that he might not see him again. 'It was really hard knowing your big brother's going out there fighting for his country and he might not come back,' George told *The X Factor*, years later. And after starting high school, sensitive George found himself the victim of cruel bullies who ended up physically hurting him, just because he didn't fit in. 'I was 12 stone and really short. All the other boys loved football and I just wanted to play my guitar. I was always the last one picked because no one wanted the fatty who couldn't run,' he told the *Daily Star Sunday*. 'The worst thing that happened was we were playing football and one of the kids purposefully kicked the ball as hard as they could right at me. I put my hands up to protect my face and ended up breaking my wrist.'

It was a nightmarish experience for George, who felt he was always a bit of a 'loner' at school. But after this traumatic experience, he transferred schools to Kings of Wessex in Cheddar, where he found his niche in the creative subjects. He even landed plum roles in school productions of *Animal Farm* and *Much Ado About Nothing* – as well as bagging his first kiss with a girl called Sandy! Meanwhile, his guitar playing went from strength to strength, and George performed in the Priddy Folk Festival near his home in Somerset, aged just 14. His dad Dominic was still an important part of his life. He spent as much time as possible at his dad's house in Nottingham, where George was accumulating even more brothers and sisters! With his new partner Rowena, George's dad Dom had three children – Leo, who came along in 2003; Archie, born in 2008, and little Spencer, born in 2011. Including George's stepsisters Annabelle and Louisa, he now had a truly huge family! George adored his little siblings and they, in turn, looked up to their cool big brother in awe.

Creative George went on to study graphic design at Weston College, part of Bath Spa University, where he received distinctions for his work. During the holidays he earned extra cash working part-time in Costa Coffee. He expected that he'd follow a career in design, perhaps in America, after graduating from uni. Meanwhile, his older half-brother Tom emigrated to Australia, where he worked as a builder but was also a drummer in a band. Seeing his eldest brother follow his musical ambitions stirred something in George. He'd long harboured a secret dream no one knew about – that he wanted to follow a career in music, too. By now, he was really talented on the guitar and was able to pick out a tune on 'anything from a bongo to a banjo', according to his mum Toni. George also had a gorgeous singing voice, but modestly held back from pushing himself forward. But a devastating event in March 2011 changed his attitude. Toni, who'd been working as a nurse, felt very ill one day and went to hospital. There, she was diagnosed with a severe migraine and sent home – whereas, actually, she was having a stroke. Toni suffered a brain bleed, which left her with loss of feeling on her left side. She had to have surgery on her wrists as well after she developed Carpal Tunnel Syndrome, a painful condition where the hands and fingers develop a dull ache and tingling sensation after a nerve is compressed. Having to leave her job and spend months recovering from a big health scare was traumatic for Toni and the rest of the family. Seeing his mum go through such a scary illness left its mark on George and he knew then that he should follow his heart.

Just a few months later, he was hanging out with Weston College friend Emily Tollner when they saw that *The X Factor* auditions would be coming to Cardiff. 'Go on,' urged Emily – it would be just a short journey away across the River Severn. Her encouraging words gave George the confidence boost he needed. And so, on a March day in 2012, he packed up his guitar, bought a train ticket and plucked up the courage. He was going to enter *The X Factor*.

CHAPTER 2

CHASING THE DREAM: THE X FACTOR AUDITIONS

The X Factor is the biggest show on UK television. Before
then, Britain had had singing contests, like *Pop Stars* and
Pop Idol – which Will Young won back in 2002 – but
nothing quite like *The X Factor* had ever been seen before.
From the moment the series hit TV screens in 2004, it
became the biggest deal going. Millions of viewers tuned
into the four-month-long series each year, which offered a
million-pound record contract to the winner. Anyone over
16 could enter and have their chance of singing their way to
superstardom. And thousands upon thousands did – in 2006
an incredible 200,000 wannabes auditioned for the show. By
the time Union J were ready for their bite at the *X Factor*
cherry, the show had made stars out of many of the winners
– including Leona Lewis, Alexandra Burke and Matt Cardle.
Even those who hadn't won the big prize found that *X Factor*
exposure in front of millions of the viewing public had
transformed their lives. JLS, Olly Murs, Stacey Solomon,
Rebecca Ferguson and even joke band Jedward had all
become hugely successful following their involvement in the
show, but in 2012 the name on everyone's lips was One
Direction.

The five-piece boyband had been put together by *The X Factor* in 2010, after originally auditioning as solo singers. They ended up coming third overall, behind Rebecca Ferguson and outright winner Matt Cardle. But since then their success had eclipsed everyone's wildest expectations. Not only did their debut single, 'What Makes You Beautiful', shoot to Number One in the UK, it went on to become an enormous hit in the US, too. With their debut album, *Up All Night*, selling in its millions across the globe, the boys were famous worldwide. They had become the first British group in American chart history to hit Number One with their debut album when it was released over there in March 2012 – and entered into the Guinness World Records as a result. As the boys from Triple J and George Shelley separately travelled to their first *X Factor* auditions, the papers and internet were full of One Direction's international success. They internet truly global superstars, and their journey had begun this same way just two years before: travelling to an *X Factor* audition alongside thousands of other hungry would-be superstars. In the back of their minds the boys must have wondered if this would end up being their big break – Josh and Jaymi in particular, as they'd been in a few boybands in the past that hadn't worked out. Would Triple J be the answer? They hoped and prayed it would be.

Behind the success of the *X Factor* lay Simon Cowell – the music-mogul-turned-reality-show-TV-judge. He'd come up with the idea after becoming famous in the UK through *Pop Idol*, and had turned *The X Factor* into the global brand it was. Notorious for his plain speaking and harsh put-downs of singers he felt were not up to scratch, Simon's pantomimebaddie act hid a sharp business brain. He was a millionaire many times over thanks to his production company owning *The X Factor* and signing the winners to his own record label, Syco. The British public had a love/hate relationship with Cowell, but it was obvious that he had the magic touch with *The X Factor*. He had appeared as the main judge on the show since its start, originally alongside music managers Louis Walsh and Sharon Osbourne. Australian singer Dannii Minogue had been brought in as a fourth judge in 2007, and her fiery relationship with Sharon saw the wife of rocker Ozzy Osbourne leave the next year – to be replaced by Cheryl Cole. This proved an amazing move for the Girls Aloud star, who became the nation's sweetheart and also launched her own top solo career. But following the launch of *The X Factor USA* in 2010, both Simon and Cheryl left the show, followed by Dannii, who was focusing on her career in Australia. It was a big shock – three-quarters of the show's judges had left. They were replaced by Take That's star singer and songwriter Gary Barlow, N-Dubz singer Tulisa Contostavlos and Destiny's Child's Kelly Rowland. With this brand-new line-up, the 2011 series of *The X Factor* faced more criticisms and controversies than usual, as viewers adjusted to this big change in the format. And it didn't work out 100 per cent successfully, as ratings dropped from the last series in 2010, which had seen an amazing 19.4 million viewers tune in for the final.

Both Triple J and George had made it through the first, early rounds of auditions, which were held without the famous judges being present. Luckily for Josh, Jaymi and JJ, this was the first year when acts with management deals were able to audition – in previous years they would have been prevented from entering. Now, in May 2012, they were heading for the judges' auditions, held in huge arenas with an audience of thousands – and filmed by the TV cameras. It was a thrilling moment for the boys – but *The X Factor* was in turmoil. Gary, Tulisa and Louis – the only judge to remain in the series since it started – had all returned to the show, but Kelly Rowland had decided not to. The papers were full of speculation as to who might be replacing her – with names like Frankie from The Saturdays, Alesha Dixon and even Katy Perry being mentioned. But no one as yet had been signed as the new permanent fourth judge and instead a raft of 'guest judges' was lined up to appear. There was a chance that one of those judges could end up being a permanent fixture.

So, it was in front of Gary, Tulisa, Louis and pop star Rita Ora that a nervous line-up of three singers appeared on that fateful day. Wearing matching outfits of tan trousers, white T-shirts and trainers, and with their *X Factor* contestant stickers plastered over them, Triple J stepped out to immediate cheers and whistles from the audience at the O2 Arena. 'Hello London!' shouted Josh, whose hair was styled in a flat side-parting. 'We're Triple J!' 'And who's with you today?' asked Louis. 'All our mums are backstage,' indicated Jaymi, who wore a buttoned-up denim shirt over his T-shirt. 'They're more nervous than us, I think,' joked Josh, to a ripple of laughter. 'Off you go,' said Louis. Triple J's big moment had arrived.

The boys launched into a rendition of Rihanna's 'We Found Love'. With their tight harmonies, well-practised vocals and confident stage presence, they were an immediate hit. With Josh taking the lead vocals, standing in the centre, and Jaymi and Josh providing perfect back-up, they were cool, relaxed and impressive. The judges raised their eyebrows in surprise, and Gary sat with a stunned smile on his face. Rita Ora bobbed her head along in time with the music. After watching a succession of disappointing acts over-promising and under-delivering, with the weird and wacky in there too, the judges looked delighted to be finally in front of an act displaying real musical talent.

Josh visibly breathed out in relief as the boys finished their song. They'd given it their all and, going by the rapturous reception from the audience, it had gone down well. But what would the judges think? Tulisa was impressed, pronouncing Triple J as the sort of boyband she liked – and that they were handsome boys, too. Josh pumped his fist in a 'Yeah!' Pop star Rita agreed, reckoning they'd be popular with a female fan base. With his years of success in Take That, first as a 1990s manufactured pop group and then with their resurgence in the last few years, older, wiser and with more hits than ever, Gary was the don of boybands. He shared his wisdom with Triple J, that they couldn't just look the part, they had to have strong vocals too, and that they'd succeeded on that front. They couldn't believe it and clasped each other's shoulders as an emotional Jaymi wiped away a tear. It was four yeses from all the judges – a full house. Triple J pumped their fists with joy and ran off the stage, leaping about. Shouting and yelling their good news, they rushed backstage, where their families were waiting anxiously alongside presenter Dermot O'Leary. Giving them all bear hugs, they shared the good news – they were through to Bootcamp.

Unlike Triple J, George Shelley didn't have the support of bandmates to boost him up as he walked onto the stage for his huge moment. The sweet 18-year-old looked terrified as he faced the biggest audience he'd ever performed in front of. Wearing a denim hoodie and beige trousers, and carrying his beloved guitar, he not only looked similarly dressed to Triple J, but his gorgeous looks also won the immediate attention and cheers of the audience. Tulisa quizzed the young singer about what he was up to in his life and George explained that he had a job in a coffee shop. Her next question was the crucial one: what was he going to sing to try to impress the judges. His answer wasn't what anyone was expecting – it was 'Toxic' by Britney Spears. It was an unusual choice – here was a teenage boy with an acoustic guitar, about to sing an electro-pop tune by a female superstar. Tulisa's surprise was written all over her face as she urged him to start. It was clear she wasn't quite expecting what was about to happen.

George went for it. Turning 'Toxic' into a quirky, up-tempo folky number, he was clearly a talented act. His voice was strong and confident as he won over the audience and played guitar expertly – all those hours of practice in his bedroom had paid off. Louis Walsh grinned through the performance, and the audience erupted in cheers as he finished. George gave a nervous half-smile as he awaited the verdict. The crowd loved it, and he could only pray the judges did, too. Louis was first in with the praise, highlighting George's terrific voice and cute face. Gary was in with a yes, too, which Tulisa added to with another positive comment – he had definitely won the judges over. An overwhelmed George put his hands over his eyes as he grinned disbelievingly. It was straight offstage and back to his mum Toni, waiting patiently behind the scenes, for a big hug. He hadn't told his family about his audition for the show at the beginning, being too shy to confess what he was doing. But since then he'd told his mum and family everything, and now they were there for his life-changing moment. This summer would be different from all the others so far – he was off to Bootcamp.

Olympic fever was about to hit the UK in that summer of 2012, and so for the first time ever Bootcamp would be held outside London, which was hosting the Games. Instead, *The X Factor* was heading for Liverpool for the serious business of auditioning the acts even further. Solo star and ex-Pussycat Doll Nicole Scherzinger had been confirmed as the permanent replacement for Kelly Rowland, and all four judges were determined that this year they would find the 'next big international superstar'. The atmosphere was charged with tension and expectation. This would be an intense three days, where the 211 acts who'd got through to Bootcamp would be whittled down to just 25, who would then be going to Judges' Houses. It was tough. Sixty acts didn't even get the chance to sing again, being sent home from Bootcamp right at the start, their dreams destroyed without a second chance. There was no room for mistakes, or to let nerves take over. Every act there had to be at the top of their game.

In this hothouse environment, there was plenty of rivalry going on behind the scenes – everyone there knew that the person next to them might knock them out of the competition. But there were also friendships being forged, too – and one of them was between Triple J and George Shelley, who had met there for the first time. The three members of Triple J spotted the 18-year-old with the guitar and walked over to introduce themselves and to ask George to sing for them. 'We bonded really, really strongly with George,' Jaymi told *This Morning* many months later. For his own part, George hit it off big time with the friendly guys from Triple J and began wishing that he could become part of a band himself. 'I came into *X Factor* hoping to be put into a group scenario,' he said. 'Especially after my first audition, I felt like I needed something around me.'

George's hopes were raised when at Bootcamp he was put in a mixed band alongside fellow contestants Charlie Cammish and Meg O'Neill for the next stage of auditions. But despite a strong rendition of Labrinth's 'Earthquake', it didn't work out and George was sent home. It was a crushing disappointment – but at least he could take comfort from the fact that he'd got through so far on his first attempt. And he'd made some great friends, leaving Liverpool with Triple J's numbers keyed into his mobile phone. Still, for George, it was back to his ordinary life, back to working as a barista in Costa Coffee and looking forward to the next uni term start-ing in September. He couldn't help but imagine, however, what might have happened if he'd made it through.

Meanwhile, Triple J endured their own marathon to make it through to Judges' Houses. They came on stage to perform their first song in front of the full panel of Nicole, Tulisa, Gary and Louis – and, of course, a huge cheering audience of thousands in Liverpool's Echo Arena. Looking full of excitement and anticipation, and almost like a real pop group, JJ, Jaymi and Josh greeted Nicole. The upfront star wanted to know why these three boys thought they deserved to win. Already showing the leadership qualities that would see him become the 'dad' of Union J in the months to come, Jaymi spoke up, promising that Triple J weren't like other boybands currently on the scene – they were unique. With fighting talk like that, the boys would have to impress.

They launched into a surprising song – a rendition of Guns N' Roses' 'Sweet Child o' Mine'. Usually a full-on rock track not known for its melodious vocals, the Triple J boys turned it into a tightly harmonised number, walking around the stage and showcasing the confidence they had with each other. For the first time, Jaymi's vocals came to the fore and he impressed the audience with his powerful, clear voice. Nicole thanked the boys for their performance, as JJ, Josh and Jaymi walked offstage into the audience and a huge cheering reception. The judges liked Triple J, but competition was beyond fierce to land a coveted spot at Judges' Houses. They had to consider who was going through and who would be competing against them. Already, another group was standing out as one to watch as well as Triple J – another three-piece called GMD3.

The judges decided to put them head-to-head in the next stage of Bootcamp, where both groups would be singing 'Moves Like Jagger' at the same time. Louis prepped the two groups for their big moment before starting proceedings. As the familiar whistling introduction to the hit Maroon 5 song began, Triple J were stunned to see GMD3 start by doing backflips. It was a slick move that impressed the judges straight away – Triple J would have to make their vocals even more bang-on to compare with that. They gave it their all and sang their hearts out, but just halfway through the song, Gary raised his hands to bring them all to a stop. Louis explained what was happening – the judges were ready to confer. The Triple J boys huddled together as they strained to hear what the judges were saying beneath their breath. Gary was of the opinion that both bands were better than before, and Nicole and Louis were particularly impressed with one band, whose members had really left an impression on them. But who were they talking about, and who would be put through to the next stage?

Wearing a stripy grey shirt, Jaymi looked pained as he clasped his hands together and waited with the other two boys to hear the verdict. Louis revealed that the judges had come to a decision and that the band coming back tomorrow would be GMD3. Was this the end of Triple J's dreams? They watched the other group happily leave the stage. Triple J pulled together, their hearts beating fiercely. But Louis wasn't finished with his big reveal – Triple J would also be returning to the auditions tomorrow! Josh yelled in delight and the others gasped in disbelief. They vowed to the judges that they would give it their best and thanked them from the bottom of their hearts. Yet again, they ran offstage on a complete high, buzzing with possibility.

As Triple J inched their way through Bootcamp, there was one more final hurdle standing between them and Judges' Houses. The standard of groups that year was high and already the judges had put a number of acts through – MK1, Times Red, Rough Copy, Mitsotu, Poisonous Twins and Duke. Now there was only one space left for another group and the judges were divided. They could see the merits of both Triple J and

GMD3 and so reluctantly came to a harsh solution. Gathering both groups onstage, Gary broke the news, looking serious. He explained that, unbelievably, Triple J would again be pitched against GMD3 for the last remaining spot. Both groups would have to sing a cappella – without any backing track – and show the judges just how good they were. With only a minute to decide their song, Jaymi gripped his stomach with nerves, while Josh and JJ looked dumbstruck.

Adrenalin rushed through their veins as Triple J frantically discussed their song choice and tried to practise as much as they could in the few seconds available to them. As they were passed three microphones, Jaymi rubbed his face, the stress clear for all to see. Taking swigs of much-needed water, Josh urged his bandmates to do anything but make a mistake. Gary signalled that the time was right to begin and that it was Triple J first. The boys launched into a harmonious version of Chris Brown's party anthem 'Yeah 3x'. It was a clean, sharp version and GMD3 looked pale with nerves as they stared across at their rivals. Gary thanked the band sincerely, as the boys put their arms around each other. The next few minutes would be agony.

GMD3 chose to sing 'Bless the Broken Road' by country singer Rascal Flatts. Their vocals were sweet and perfectly in tune – Jaymi looked across, impressed by the other group. Josh crossed his arms, a deadly serious look on his face. GMD3 were storming it and there was no chance Triple J would be the clear winners in this sing-off. Although they tried to keep their expressions neutral, the judges were evidently impressed – especially Tulisa, who sat with her chin in her hands, gazing up at GMD3. They ended with a perfectly delivered melisma (packing a series of different notes into a single syllable) – it had been a great performance. Gary thanked the groups and asked for a few moments to make their decisions. The judges conferred again, with Nicole voicing her concerns that both groups were deserving of the spot. But it sounded as if there was no doubt in Tulisa's mind, as she praised one particular group for moving her. With their eyes red-rimmed with tears, JJ, Jaymi and Josh pulled together to hear their fate.

Gary was apologetic as he delivered their verdict. Accepting that they had always been pitched against each other, it was going to be a hard moment when just one of GMD3 or Triple J would see it through to Judges' Houses. And the name on his lips was … GMD3. That was it – Triple J were out! The tension and anxiety that had been rushing through them these past few days suddenly left, and the boys came back down to earth with a bump. Turning to congratulate their fellow group, the boys were resigned but grateful for the experience. Jaymi turned to mouth 'thank you' to the judges. Gary congratulated Triple J for their hard work, looking genuinely devastated to be sending home the three talented boys. They stumbled offstage in shock, with Jaymi only managing to utter a few words about how good GMD3 had been to a waiting Dermot. Josh's emotions had overcome him and he was by now in floods of tears. Ever the optimist, Jaymi told the waiting cameras that this wouldn't be the end of the band – they were still going to chase their dream of pop success.

It had been their best shot, but now Triple J had been kicked out of *The X Factor*. As Josh, Jaymi and JJ gathered their bags and began the long journey home, they tried to come to terms with the crushing blow just dealt them. Perhaps Triple J wasn't meant to be. And the fact was, it wasn't. But though the boys didn't know it then, soon enough they would be back on *The X Factor* – in an incredible twist to their line-up and name that would leave everyone amazed.

CHAPTER 3

MEET UNION J: COMEBACK AT THE JUDGES' HOUSES

It was just an ordinary summer's night for George Shelley when a phone call arrived that would change his life forever. The teenager was sitting at home in Clevedon, chatting with his mum, when his mobile rang. It had been a few weeks since George had suffered the disappointment of not making it through the Bootcamp phase of *The X Factor*, but he'd managed to put it to the back of his mind. Instead, he was focusing on going back to uni and moving on with his life. But as George's mum Toni watched her son's face go 'taut' as he took the phone call, she knew something was up. 'It's *The X Factor* on the phone,' George mouthed at her, stunned. Indeed, it was one of the show's producers, who asked if George would be interested in returning to the show. Circumstances had changed and they were now keen to see the talented West Country teenager once more. George couldn't believe it. As he put the phone down, he explained to his mum: 'I've got an hour to call them back with my decision. If I agree to go back, I've got to be in London tomorrow morning!'

It was a no-brainer – George and his mum decided to go to London for this out-of-the-blue opportunity. George didn't know it then, but behind the scenes there had been a lot of interest in him since he'd left *The X Factor*, and the stars were about to align in his favour.

Triple J's manager Blair Dreelan had spotted the handsome singer at Bootcamp and thought he had the potential to be developed into a solo star. After getting George's details, he stayed in touch with him and decided to manage him – but then, spookily, *The X Factor* producers also contacted Blair about Triple J returning to the competition. Incredibly, a last-minute slot had opened up due to a visa issue with one of the groups, South London's Rough Copy. The Judges' Houses episodes were to be filmed mainly abroad, so Nigerian-born member Kazeem Ajobo had to apply for a visa to travel to the United States and then back to the UK. Unfortunately for Rough Copy, the application hadn't been approved in time, so the band wouldn't be able to travel and take part in the show. With days to go before filming was required to start, *The X Factor* producers convened an emergency meeting with Louis Walsh – who was to be the Groups mentor – to discuss who could replace Rough Copy. There were two groups who'd stood out in the Irish mogul's eyes: Triple J and Times Red. 'When Rough Copy left, I found it difficult to choose between two groups to fill their place. In the end, I invited boyband Triple J to come to Judges' Houses, but still felt that, as I'd lost such a strong group in Rough Copy, I wanted to make sure the category was the best it could possibly be,' he told the *Mirror*. 'I asked Gary, Nicole and Tulisa if they minded if I took a seventh act. They were happy as they felt they'd got the right six acts for their

Judges' Houses trips, so I asked Times Red to come along and they said yes.'

Producers quickly got in touch with Blair Dreelan to see if Triple J would be able to return to *The X Factor* – but they had another suggestion as well. Louis had felt that the band would benefit from adding another member to the line-up, and they already had someone in mind. Blair explained to Sugarscape.com that *The X Factor* suggested putting a fourth member into his group. Initially unsure of this idea, Blair was amazed when producers told him who they were thinking of to take this fourth spot. It was the same George Shelley that he knew and was now managing – what were the chances in a competition where 180,000 people had auditioned? It seemed like fate to Blair and so he accepted their suggestion.

The X Factor and Blair prepped the Triple J boys for what was about to happen – they were going to become a four-piece! The boys were chuffed – after all, they'd met George at Bootcamp and already hit it off with him. Jaymi had even shown Blair a picture of George, telling him how he thought he looked amazing. He'd then used his computer skills to scan in George to a line-up of Triple J, unwittingly predicting what would really happen to the band in real life when they became Union J. Triple J's manager sensed that their personalities would mesh well, but with only a few days before they were due to go to Judges' Houses, time was of the essence. The boys spent the next four days getting to know each other and practising their singing for the competition. It was a whirlwind time: just a few days before, they had thought their *X Factor* dreams were finished, and now they were about to return for a second chance at a place in the live shows with an extra member, in a doubly shocking twist.

It was a thrilling time for the newly formed band, who hit it off as a foursome straight away. 'When they suggested it, it made sense,' the boys told *We Love Pop* magazine. 'When George came along, it wasn't a big deal, as we were literally all so new to each other anyway.' It was a second chance at *The X Factor* that none of them had been expecting after their bruising Bootcamp experience, and they were ready to take it on. After telling their families this exciting news, the boys began packing for the mystery destination. But one more thing needed to be sorted out before they could leave: a new name. Obviously, they couldn't be 'Triple J' any more. Instead, the boys put their heads together and came up with an idea – they would take the name 'Union Jack' and shorten it to 'Union J', representing all their names. Although George's name began with a G, it had a similar sound. As Jaymi pointed out later, even when they tried to change it to the Spanish spelling of George – Jorge – it wouldn't work, because that was pronounced 'Hor-hay'! And so Union J were born and they immediately released their first state-ment to the media. 'We couldn't believe it when we got the call about going to Judges' Houses, and of course we jumped at the chance,' they said. 'It's a once-in-a-lifetime opportu-nity. We're so happy to be a four-piece, too. The group feels so right together – it feels like we've been together for years!'

It was time for the groups to discover who was to mentor them and where they were going. Firstly, waiting at the airport, they discovered their destination – Las Vegas! The boys and the six other groups boarded their plane and spent the long journey across the Atlantic full of nerves and expectation. However, they also used the time to their advantage, practising harmonies and singing – after all, they'd only had a few days together so far, and this was an incredible opportunity to potentially make their dreams come true. Arriving in the dazzling American city, they all headed to Caesars Palace hotel and casino to find out who was going to mentor them. Pulling up in a white stretch limo, it was Louis Walsh! The longest-serving *X Factor* judge, Louis was also a seasoned manager of boybands, having driven both Boyzone and Westlife to huge success. He explained to the waiting wannabes that although there were seven of them in front of him, there was only room on the show for three acts – less than 50 per cent. The bands making it through would be the ones who impressed Louis by committing themselves fully to the competition the next day. Accompanying him was Sharon Osbourne, the former *X Factor* judge and a renowned music manager in her own right. Her advice was also deadly serious – the groups there had the chance for the biggest break of their life. In the setting of Las Vegas, where superstars from around the world performed, they had a once-in-a-lifetime opportunity. As if the groups needed reminding. Meanwhile, the other acts gathered in different corners of the globe to sing for their lives. Gary Barlow was at the grand Boughton House in Northamptonshire with the Over-28s, where Cheryl Cole came to offer advice. Nicole Scherzinger took her Boys to Dubai, with Ne-Yo as her second-in-command. Lastly, Tulisa took her Girls all the way to St Lucia, where Tinie Tempah helped her choose.

But for Union J over in Nevada, there wasn't any time to relax in the opulent surroundings of their hotel or to enjoy the thrills of the Las Vegas Strip – soon they would perform for the first time ever as a group, and this performance was to seal their fate for good. Now the pressure was on more than ever. George could barely comprehend that in just ten minutes, they would be performing in front of the judges. As the boys sat in the hotel, Jaymi mused on the turnaround in their fortunes – just a few days ago they hadn't even been together as a four-piece and now they had the chance to make it happen. It was clear they were still overwhelmed by what had happened to them. Fortunately the boys had bonded very quickly and, despite going through a 'roller-coaster' four days, they already knew that they had a brilliant rapport. They were so tightly connected, they felt like brothers. Although Triple J had been a great group, Jaymi knew that as a four-piece they could take on the world.

Finally, the boys strolled down the steps onto the hotel rooftop. It was night-time and the shimmering lights of Las Vegas below proved a dramatic backdrop to Union J's first ever performance. Louis and Sharon sat forward on a luxurious white sofa, keen to listen as the boys, dressed for the warm weather in T-shirts and long shorts, steeled themselves. Louis quizzed the boys on what this chance would mean to them – if they made it through. Josh earnestly declared that it would be the best thing ever – returning home after their last disappointment had been crushing. Now they had a second chance at their dream. George shook his head, trying to take in this surreal situation. It was time for Union J to perform as Louis asked them to start.

This was their moment. George began gently strumming his guitar and Josh started singing the first few bars of Carly Rae Jepsen's 'Call Me Maybe', an up-tempo dance track that had been everywhere in 2012. The boys slowed it right down and turned it into a sweet, romantic song, complete with stunning harmonies. Louis and Sharon leaned forward on their sofa, ears pricked up once they realised they were hearing something special. As the boys got into the song, their confidence grew and they started to smile and enjoy themselves. This positivity proved infectious and the savvy, seen-it-all-before Sharon began to smile as well. She and Louis looked at each other and nodded – this was going well. Louis thanked the group as the boys finished, sounding surprised at how faultlessly this brand-new boyband had performed together. Dermot O'Leary, who was waiting for Union J to the side, wanted to know how it had been for them. George was stunned and could barely get the words out, but explained briefly that it had been very affecting. Meanwhile, Louis and Sharon were discussing the boys, but it wasn't a 100 per cent glowing reception. Sharon noted that a couple of the boys – she didn't say who – had developed amateur tics with their delivery and performance. But Louis insisted that they had the potential to be much, much better if they worked hard. The boys returned later to sing their second song – 'Forever Young' by Mr Hudson – and delivered another impressive rendition, with perfect harmonies and Jaymi showcasing his powerful voice. Afterwards, talking to Caroline Flack on *The Xtra Factor*, it was evident that Union J were loving singing as a four. JJ enthusiastically agreed that, aside from their nerves, it had been a brilliant experience.

But it wouldn't be long before they learned their fate. The next morning, the four boys were up on the hotel rooftop again, waiting to hear Louis's verdict. The hot sun beat down on them, intensifying the tension that they undoubtedly felt. For them, it was a strange feeling of déjà vu, as they prayed that this time they would hear good news. An emotional Jaymi couldn't bear the thought of having yet another no after so many disappointments. Josh agreed, saying that they craved for this band to work and were prepared to give it their all. After going through such ups and downs over the past few weeks in their *X Factor* journey, the boys knew that a second rejection would hurt twice as much as the first. Jaymi knew that there was a reason they'd been brought back – the kernel of something special had been spotted in them. Another rejection would be awful. Pacing around the hotel roof, with the dramatic mountain backdrop behind them, Josh tried to steady his breath. He worried about the impact on his nearest and dearest, aware that he'd been through so many near-misses before. George patted his chest as his heart raced, and then put a comforting arm around Josh's shoulder as the emotion got to him. It was a sickening moment for every single lad.

Louis opened proceedings with a compliment, praising their first audition, as the Union J boys stood in a line in front of him, George biting his fingers nervously. Louis went on to explain that, as Jaymi thought, there was potential for the group to be great. Louis had taken a chance by putting George into the mix and he was pleased with how things were going. But – and it was a big but – Louis wasn't sure there was enough time to get Union J show-ready. After all, they hadn't been together long. Red-eyed and on the edge, Union J prayed that this didn't mean Louis thought they were a lost cause. They knew they would work harder than they'd ever worked before if only they got this chance. As they pulled together, arms around each other, they listened to Louis continuing his appraisal. Soon, Louis appeared to confirm their worst fears by highlighting the other boybands in the competition — with their increased experience they had an advantage over the newbies, Union J. Josh tensed his jaw and JJ's mouth dropped open in shock — they thought it was all over. As Jaymi gazed at the floor, he wiped away tears. Now it was time for Louis to make his decision. He explained to the boys that he didn't like taking chances. As JJ silently mouthed please under his breath, Louis delivered his smash. He was ready to take a chance right now. It was an unexpected twist — the boys all raised their heads in a sudden burst of hope. It was true — they were through!

It was the culmination of months — and years — of dashed hopes. Union J cheered with joy like they'd never cheered before, and immediately ran towards Louis in utter elation. As JJ, Jaymi and George pushed Louis onto the sofa for a bear hug, Josh collapsed onto his knees, unable to take in the incredible news they'd just heard. The four boys then ran into a group hug, shouting 'Yes!' and hiccupping with the emotion of the moment. They could hardly gather themselves, as Louis, breathing out a sigh of relief, tried to regain order. He warned the boys that the difficult phase was just starting — they were surrounded by rivals who were all as hungry for the *X Factor* crown as they were. JJ sobbed, and declared his loyalty to the judge. The boys had never felt like this before.

In the space of a couple of weeks, their fortunes had turned around by 180 degrees and now they would be taking part in the *X Factor* finals – the biggest platform for a pop group on British TV. Louis laughed as he made sure the boys knew that they had to demonstrate that they were worth this chance. The bandmates ran off in hysterical happiness. They yelled and shouted about their good fortune as they pulled each other into another tight hug. Flying back to Britain after such an incredible few days, they couldn't wait to tell their families, who had no idea what had happened yet. They sat at Gatwick Airport, nervously waiting for the boys to return, all the while hoping they'd be coming back with good news. 'We were all there sitting in Costa Coffee, waiting for the contestants to get off the plane,' explained Toni, George's mum. 'We still, at that stage, didn't know whether they had got through. But then I saw George and he shouted "Yes!" and then there was lots of hugging and kissing.'

What a moment for Union J – their lives would never be the same again. After believing their *X Factor* dreams were over, they were now through to the finals, which would come to determine the course of their futures forever. Despite their jubilation, Union J knew there was more hard work to come. They now faced the toughest competition of their lives as the judges selected the other finalists. Turning down Times Red – who, like Union J, had been given a second chance at Judges' Houses – Louis instead selected MK1, an urban hip-hop duo from East London, and GMD3, the vocal harmony three-piece boyband that had previously defeated Union J at Bootcamp. Nicole Scherzinger had selected her three boys: firstly, James Arthur, a talented guitarist and singer from Saltburn, Teeside, alongside Jahmene Douglas, a shy singer from Birmingham with an astonishing voice. Rounding out her trio was Rylan Clark – a controversial entry, as the out-there model and actor from Essex had bags of charisma but didn't have the strongest voice. Meanwhile, Gary Barlow had chosen his Over-28s. They were Carolynne Poole, a talented singer from Yorkshire who'd been booted out at Judges' Houses the year before by Louis; former chimney sweep Kye Sones from Pinner, Northwest London, and Melanie Masson, a children's entertainer from Glasgow. Lastly, Tulisa had chosen an amazing group of girls for the live finals: Lucy Spraggan, a quirky guitarist and singer from Buxton who'd already hit the charts with her self-penned *X Factor* audition song, 'Last Night'; Ella Henderson, a 16-year-old with an incredible voice, and Jade Ellis, a talented singer from Southeast London who oozed star attitude.

A wildly different bunch, they would now be pitted directly against each other in the bear pit of the *X Factor* finals. Now not only the judges but also the voting public would have their say – and so, too, would the media. Union J were about to embark on the ride of their lives.

CHAPTER 4

GOING LIVE! THE LIVE SHOWS, WEEK ONE

They were through to the live shows. Finally, the weeks and months of nervous auditioning had resulted in a dream come true – the boys would be taking part in the biggest, most exciting part of *The X Factor* – the week-by-week phase where they performed live to the nation. Now they were part of the legendary 'Final 12'. If they thought life had taken a twist in a crazy direction before, they were about to become fully fledged TV superstars, with millions of viewers watching them each week to decide their fate. Would they win over the British public and become the new hot boyband on everyone's lips, set for storming chart success? Or would they fall at the first hurdle and be voted out straight away, disappearing without trace? At this stage, no one could predict what would happen, but the sheer thrill of being on the show was driving Union J on. Speaking backstage on *The X Factor* as they recorded the first of their behind-the-scenes interviews, their amazement and happiness shone through.

Firstly, it was time to move into *X Factor* World full time. In previous years of the show, the finalists had all lived together in a big house rented by the show and located in a suburb of London. This had sometimes caused problems, with neighbours complaining about the hordes of screaming fans congregated outside on the road! So, this year, the show's producers made a decision – the finalists would move into a hotel. But not just any old place; this was the five-star Corinthia Hotel – a favourite of Rihanna, which dazzled them all with its luxurious glamour. With the hotel located slap-bang in the centre of London, just a short walk away from both the Prime Minister's home at 10 Downing Street and the Royal Family's residence at Buckingham Palace, this year's contestants were in the thick of the action in Britain's buzzing capital. Each of them would be staying in rooms that cost £500 a night, complete with flat-screen TV in both the room and the bath, rain-dance shower, sumptuous beds and full access to the gym and spa. It was certainly a leap into the big time and a taster of what their life might be like should *X Factor* final success come their way. Pulling up outside their impressive new home for the next few weeks, the Union J boys couldn't believe it. Josh even joked to the cameras that this place left his own home in the shade as they walked up the grand steps. Entering their plush new room, George leapt on a bed, claiming the best spot for himself. But the other boys weren't going to let cheeky George have his way straight away – they laughed as they jumped on the bed too, amazed at their incredible good fortune. This was going to be fun.

But it wasn't all to be the life of a pampered A-list super-star from now on. There was a lot of work ahead needed to turn the boys into fully fledged pop stars – and there would be rules to follow, too. Almost straight away, the contestants had the mini-bars taken out of their rooms, after Staz Nair from Times Red ended up running naked down a corridor.

'The contestants have been spoiled with their accommodation and are being waited on hand and foot – but bosses can't foot the bar bill, especially if they're going to sink the amount of booze they're clearly capable of,' reported the *Sun*. It was clear that the *X Factor* producers were not prepared to have bad behaviour giving the show a poor reputation with the other swanky guests. And the Union J boys found that the live shows meant a whole new level of grooming was required, despite their already gorgeous looks. 'We've had [our] eyebrows done, haircuts, facials – we're getting the star treatment we're not really used to,' said George. Stylists also had a field day with Josh – completely restyling his hair and turning the sideswept fringe into a 1950s-style quiff that showed off his incredible cheekbones and piercing eyes. Little did they know this was only the beginning.

As the nation counted down the days till the first live show, it was time for Union J to dip their toes into the big world of publicity. Soon, they would be old hands at giving interviews to magazines, websites, radio and TV stations, but at this stage it was still new – and nerve-wracking. Alongside Louis and the other groups, MK1 and GMD3 (who hadn't yet changed their name to District 3), they appeared on ITV's *This Morning*. Laughing at his own ignorance of who was who, presenter Eamonn Holmes showed the guests the picture card he'd been given to help him identify these as yet unknown wannabe pop stars. 'When you're all famous, look back on this very moment,' he told them. Josh was one of the first to speak up about how much the experience meant to them. 'Watching the show every year, being a fan … and now we're on the show, it's amazing for all of us,' he said. Fellow

presenter Ruth Langsford wanted to know how it was starting off now as a four-piece, when they'd not made it through
Bootcamp as a threesome. 'We went home to our normal
jobs and it was gutting,' explained Jaymi. 'Then Louis came
round and explained there'd been a problem with one of the
groups and they were going to offer us a place at Judges'
Houses,' added George.' 'What was that like?' asked Ruth.
Jaymi explained how quickly they'd bonded, despite the last-
minute situation: 'He fitted in straight away. When we both
came out of the competition we stayed in contact. We were
thinking of joining up as a group anyway, so we love having
him.' And George agreed. 'Especially after my first audition
– I felt like I wanted someone else around me, so I'd been
hoping I would be put in a group,' he said. The lads also
appeared on ITV's *Daybreak*, where Josh talked enthusiastically about how George had seamlessly blended into the
band. 'It's been awesome, he's fitted in straight away – he's
one of us now,' he said, smiling. He then revealed how
anxious he felt about the upcoming live shows. 'I've got
every single emotion inside me: nervous, excited, scared,
terrified, buzzing – everything! I can't wait.'

Despite the boys' nerves at the prospect of the first week
performing live, their mentor Louis was right behind them.
He was thrilled to have a group of lads that had the magic
quality of good looks and great voices. He knew that they
would garner fans immediately. Getting ready for the first
week's show also entailed plenty of hard work; the boys had
intensive vocal and dance coaching. Performing each week
on the biggest show going meant standards needed to be as
high as they possibly could be, and Union J were putting in

the hours of hard graft required. *The X Factor*'s creative director, Brian Friedman, has choreographed the dance routines of some of the world's biggest pop acts, including Britney Spears and *NSYNC. He helped the boys craft their routines, and made sure they understood the message they had to get across to their fans. Brian explained that if they were going to be called 'Union J' their image had to be all about sticking together as a four, which could be expressed in their choreography.

Of course, this was the other reason why the boys felt especially nervous about their first week of live shows. Having introduced themselves to the viewers at home as Triple J, they were now a four-piece, with a new member – George – and a new name. How would the audience – and the millions watching from their living rooms at home – react to this change? It was a big risk, but Louis felt it was the right one to take. He knew that they had been missing something when it had just been the three of them – and George had provided that final spark that made them a group to be reckoned with. And there was no doubt that the boys felt the same about their new line-up. Jaymi even pronounced that George coming into the group had been an incredible moment and his fellow bandmates supported his feelings. For Josh, Triple J was becoming a distant memory, and the future was all about Union J. It felt to all of them like it had been written in the stars. The bandmates were happy with their new arrangement, laughing and joking like brothers – but would the *X Factor* fans agree? This week would be the first proper test of the new Union J.

It was nearly time for the first live show when, on the Thursday of that week, Union J took to the stage at the Fountain Studios in Wembley for the first ever dress rehearsal. There was no audience sitting there to cheer – or boo – them on, nor was there an audience at home. But still, as the reality of their situation sank in, Union J realised in a moment of harsh clarity that the standard this year of their fellow singers was amazingly high. They weren't convinced of their value – would they really be able to hold their own? Luckily, mentor Louis was on hand to give the boys a boost, making them realise they were just as worthy a competitor as all the others. And it wasn't just Louis who was giving the boys expert advice. Already, comparisons were being made between Union J and another *X Factor* boyband – One Direction. After coming third in the 2010 series, One Direction had gone on to become global superstars, and now they returned to the series that made them huge to pass on some wise words to the new kids on the block.

Josh was especially thrilled to meet the group, as they'd been just like Union J two years previously – a new band desperate to make it on *The X Factor*. Louis from One Direction had some simple words of advice to their fledgling friends when they met backstage before the show – it was important to enjoy the moment and be natural, and to let their personalities shine. After their chat, all the boys felt better, especially Jaymi, who vowed they wouldn't let down those who'd given them this vital chance.

The screams built up to a deafening level in the *X Factor* studios in Wembley, Northwest London, on the night of 6 October 2012. This was it – now there was no going back for the Union J boys. Everyone would be watching them eagerly to see if they'd be able to cut it as a new group. And not only would their family and friends be watching, there were plenty of celebrities waiting to see Union J's first public performance, too. It was Heroes night, inspired by the amazing summer Britain had just had with the London 2012 Olympic Games. The country was still buzzing from the incredible achievements of Team GB in bringing home a record-breaking 65 medals, and lots of star Olympians were in the audience. Boxer Nicola Adams, rower Tom James, taekwondo star Jade Jones and cyclists Danielle (Dani) King, Joanne Rowsell and Laura Trott were all there – Josh even made a daft joke about Laura Trott's name and her being sexy, as the others cringed with laughter. The Union J boys were singing a classic rock tune – Queen's 'Don't Stop Me Now'. Everyone knew and loved this song – but would the boys be able to make it their own and avoid elimination in the first week?

The boys went on halfway through the show – immediately after wild-card entry Christopher Maloney had performed Mariah Carey's 'Hero' to a rapturous reception, with Nicole pronouncing him fantastic. (Sadly, Times Red didn't make it through the wild-card stage, nor Amy Mattrom or Adam Burridge.) Standing together on a plinth that read 'UNION J' in huge, blue letters, George started singing the first lines on his own. Jaymi then took over and before long the boys were all singing together, jumping around the stage as if born to it. The high-energy performance whisked by incredibly fast and as the boys finished their performance, hands on each other's shoulders, no one could doubt the chemistry was right. As the audience clapped and cheered wildy, George and Jaymi especially looked overwhelmed by the reception. They'd done it!

But they were soon brought back down to earth with a bump. Tulisa was the first judge to comment, and her words were not positive. Looking devastated, she explained why she hadn't connected with the boys' performance that first night. It was the song choice – an old rock tune wasn't what she thought a young boyband should be singing. She accused Louis, their mentor, of failing his group.

The boys were stunned. After all the build-up and excitement of the first night of what they hoped was their new pop career, here was one of the judges immediately saying that they hadn't impressed her. Louis rushed to defend his song choice – declaring it an upbeat number in the vein of hit TV musical show *Glee*. He was clearly rattled that his band hadn't triumphed straight away. But Tulisa wasn't having any of this – and reiterated that she laid the blame at Louis's door. Although she didn't criticise Union J directly, the boys were crestfallen. Lined up before the judges, the looks of shock on their faces were heartbreaking.

But what about the other judges? There was no time to hope that Gary and Nicole might be thinking differently. Almost straight away, Gary chimed in, agreeing with his fellow judge Tulisa. Although he liked Union J, he again threw barbs at Louis, accusing him of making them sing a terrible track and condeming Union J to a poor start in the competition. Standing on the stage, with their hearts beating at full pelt, the Union J boys couldn't believe their ears. This wasn't going well for them at all. Suddenly, the prospect of leaving the show right at the beginning felt scarily real. But Gary wasn't done with his criticisms yet, pronouncing their version old-fashioned and cheesy. Like Tulisa, he went in for trashing Louis's judgement on boybands in the modern age. Cornered by the judges' reaction, Louis quickly switched tack and admitted he'd got the selection wrong, and perhaps choosing Queen hadn't been right for the boys and maybe they hadn't been ready to take it on yet. Tulisa and Gary started arguing with Louis and it became clear that Union J weren't having an easy ride of it on Week One – already they'd split the judges and created a row!

It came to Nicole to calm things down and point out what the boys had achieved that night. The fact that they had come onstage as Union J for the first time on British television hadn't escaped her. She congratulated the nervous quartet for an amazing achievement – they had sung live on national TV as a band. At last, a positive comment lifted the grim mood in the studio, with whoops and cheers from the audience showing that at least there were some fans rooting for Union J. But even Nicole had to agree with the other judges that the song choice hadn't been right for the band. There was no way around it – despite liking the band, she didn't like their song. So that was that – the three judges aside from their mentor Louis hadn't liked their first-week performance. All their enthusiasm and dreams for how their first week would go had been crushed. Louis brought proceedings to an end, vowing to help his protégés and that they would put in even more work next week if they were thrown a lifeline and kept in by the voting public. But would the band get a second chance?

It was time for presenter Dermot O'Leary to step in and get the boys' reactions. Quizzing them on their feelings, he pointed out that even Louis had conceded they'd sung the wrong song. Reeling from the shock, the bandmates had to confront what had happened straight away. JJ was standing next to Dermot and tried to be as positive as he could through his visible disappointment. He could barely find the words as he haltingly promised that they had tried their hardest – but would do better if they got another chance. George was up next, and the screams from girls in the audience as he began to speak demonstrated that, even at this early stage, he was fast becoming a favourite. Smiling shyly, he simply thanked the judges and assured them that they had listened to the criticisms. Over the screams, Louis echoed their sentiments, vowing to put everything they had behind the band if they could only come back the following week. He desperately didn't want them to lose out in just Week One.

As Dermot read out the phone number to vote for Union J, Josh did a nervous thumbs-up at the viewers and the audience. It was clear that they knew their future would not be secured by that performance alone. They needed the support of everyone who liked the band if they were going to stay in – but did they have enough fans at this early stage?

Union J faced a tense night back at their hotel as they waited for the Sunday-night results show. When the next day arrived, it was back to the studios and time for the show to go on. Putting their worries to one side, they joined forces with the other finalists for the opening group performance of Emeli Sandé's 'Read All About It'. But soon it was time to face the music. The boys walked on with District 3, MK1 and their mentor Louis, clearly unsure of where their fate lay. To the dramatic strains of the classical music piece 'O Fortuna' – used every year on *The X Factor* – Union J stood under the blue spotlights, heads down, waiting to hear the results. The tension was sky-high, with each finalist silently praying they wouldn't be the first to leave the show – and with it the chance of their dreams coming true.

Josh rubbed his hands nervously as they waited for the first act to be saved. It was Kye. One after the other, names were called out: James, then District 3. Union J congratulated their fellow group on making it through, but did this mean their chances were getting slimmer by the second? Ella Henderson was next, but after her incredible performance of Take That's 'Rule the World' was praised to the skies by Gary, it came as no surprise. Then Lucy Spraggan's name was called, amping up the tension for Union J even further. Would their name be called next? No, it was MK1, another member of the Groups team. By now, Union J were one of the last acts standing on the stage, and they must have thought their time was up. Melanie's name, then Jahmene's were called – this was becoming unbearable for the boys. Jaymi was biting his hands with the stress of it all, but their agony wasn't over. Jade's name was called next, and Tulisa celebrated as her last act went through from the Girls group. Then, finally, Dermot said the words they'd been willing him to utter – that the tenth act through to the next round was them! The boys went wild, screaming in delight and jumping on each other as they realised their dream wasn't over yet. It had been a close call, but in front of nine million viewers, they'd shown that they could make it through the first week.

Union J's night was finally finished, but of course there had to be one act leaving. The two left onstage were Rylan Clark and Carolynne Poole. Carolynne sang the country star Faith Hill's 'There'll Be You', her smooth and powerful voice soaring above the music. Rylan performed the *Dreamgirls'* dance track 'One Night Only' and, despite giving it his all, it became clear that his voice wasn't of the same standard as Carolynne's – cracking and even missing notes.

But the final decision was down to the judges. Nicole spoke first, and as Rylan's mentor, her loyalty was clear. She complimented Carolynne's incredibly powerful voice, but explained she had no option but to stick with her own act, sending Carolynne home. Gary was up next and supported his mentee, too. He couldn't resist a dig at Rylan, who Gary clearly didn't believe deserved a place in the finals, making a sarcastic jibe about Rylan's singing being improved when he sang away from the microphone! Of course, Gary was sending Rylan home. Tulisa was the first of the judges to make a decision not based on who was in her group. She adored Rylan and his charismatic stage presence, but in the end decided to go for sheer musicality. She was going to send Rylan home, too.

So the final decision was down to Louis – if he sent Rylan home, that was it. But it became evident very quickly that Louis was feeling conflicted. In the same sentence he praised Carolynne and Rylan for different attributes – Carolynne for her singing and Rylan for his entertaining presence. Time was running out and Dermot pressured him for a quick answer. In the background the audience chanted Rylan's name over and over again as the famous *X Factor* tension returned to the show. Louis moaned as he tried in vain to make a decision he was finding agonisingly difficult. The other judges were becoming increasingly frustrated – Gary in particular, who didn't agree with his fellow judges that Rylan brought a burst of fun and light to the competition. He was getting more and more cross as Louis vacillated.

Resting his cheek on his hands, Louis looked no closer to making a decision, even as Dermot shouted at him. Onstage, the two contestants looked sick with nerves as their fate took even longer to decide than normal. Looking on the verge of tears, it seemed for one moment that Louis had declared he was supporting Carolynne. But just as Dermot tried to confirm that he wanted to dispatch Rylan, Louis changed his mind again. He wanted them both to stay in, but that was going to be impossible. Louis had thrown the show into a state of utter confusion. By now, Dermot was at the end of his tether and urged Louis to make a choice. He did – taking it to deadlock and letting the public vote decide.

Both Rylan and Carolynne gazed at the floor in despair as the boos began to build in the studio. Gary stood up in shock and anger at his fellow judge. Union J's mentor had not got off to a good start in this series with the viewing public. As a member of the production staff handed Dermot an envelope, he explained that they would now revert to the earlier public vote. The person with the fewest number of votes had been Carolynne – so she would be the first to go. As the disappointed singer hugged Dermot, Gary walked off the judges' panel in an absolute rage. It was clear that *The X*

Factor Season Nine would not be short on controversy. And they didn't know it yet, but Union J were to be at the heart of it.

CHAPTER 5

A TASTE OF FAME:
THE LIVE SHOWS, WEEK TWO

The X Factor had certainly started its live shows with a bang – and Union J were swept up in the tabloid feeding frenzy that followed that dramatic Sunday night. The newspapers and online community buzzed with Gary's fury, as he raged backstage that Carolynne's departure from the show was ridiculous. Meanwhile, the boys' mentor, Louis, found himself at the centre of speculation that he'd been 'told' by a producer to take the vote to deadlock – something that he strongly denied. 'People are tweeting that last night was a fix, and a picture is published showing [producer] Richard talking to me,' Louis wrote in the *Daily Mail*. 'The story is that he's telling me how to vote – but that's not true. No one has ever told us what to do.' As the controversy over Rylan remaining in the competition grew, Louis was forced to explain why he brought the vote to deadlock. 'I feel totally torn after Carolynne and Rylan's performances,' he wrote. 'I like them both … I want to do the right thing. I feel like I am looking stupid, like a rabbit in the headlights, but that's the thing about *The X Factor* – it's live, it's real, anything can happen. In the end I think, oh, I'll let the public decide. I don't know which of them is going to be at the bottom on the public vote. Gary is annoyed and storms off. He hates losing, especially on the first show.'

Louis may have eventually escaped unscathed from the tabloid storm, but it left Union J in no doubt that they would have to bring much more to the show. With a talented act like Carolynne losing out to a more entertaining, divisive figure like Rylan, it showed that no one was safe. Only the full package of talent, performance and charisma would do – and the boys knew it. What's more, after the first live shows the betting companies began to release their figures on who was most likely to win. After her incredible performance of 'Rule the World', Ella Henderson was top of the table, with Paddy Power putting her at 10/11 on to win the entire competition. Union J struggled with much longer odds of 16/1. Clearly there was a lot of work to do.

At the beginning of the week, Louis sat the boys down for a stern talk about upping their game. In his office, he reiterated how fortunate they were to have this chance and to have made it through. The only thing that was going to secure their status now was hard work – and lots of it. The week would have to be filled with practising and little else if Union J were to succeed over their rivals. Individually they realised that, although they'd pulled together as a four-piece, it wouldn't be enough to survive in the cut-throat world of *The X Factor*. Josh knew that the previous week's performance hadn't really worked and, along with the other boys, had felt the dread of expecting to be sent home. If anything, this had sharpened their resolve to keep their place all the more. They were going to throw themselves entirely into becoming an incredible band,

And so the Union J boys knuckled down, spending hour upon hour each day practising their new song and routine. Work took priority over everything – even during photoshoots the boys used their brief moments of downtime to go over their moves or practise their harmonies. They even watched their first week's performance back on screen, to see what they could improve on this time round.

Dance expert Brian Friedman continued teaching them how to bring their routines more in sync – and took no prisoners with his demanding training. Shouting at them during one tiring studio rehearsal, Brian didn't let up for one second – there was no time to rest, no time for a break. Exhausted, the boys picked themselves up and started practising again.

This wasn't the fun free-for-all that they might have been expecting of the *X Factor* experience, but Union J stepped up to the plate and proved they had the ability to work hard. By Friday of that week they were done in, but satisfied they had prepared much more fully for the challenges of the weekend's shows ahead. 'We've been rehearsing like mad and focusing on the vocals,' explained Josh to presenter Pips Taylor in the TalkTalk backstage lounge – an online show which regularly interviewed the stars of the series. 'Last week was a hard song to do; it didn't really show us off vocally as much as it could have done.'

Even Louis was impressed by their efforts. He could see that his mentees had been putting in incredible amounts of work and hoped that this would be one in the eye for Gary's criticism that Louis was out of touch with boybands. Union J were determined beyond measure to prove themselves. They still hadn't forgotten how slim this window of opportunity had been for them – nearly not making it through on many occasions – and it redoubled their sense of responsibility to make Louis proud.

Meanwhile, the whole of the UK was going *X Factor* crazy. Every day brought fresh stories about the contestants and their newfound fame. Poor Lucy Spraggan had to deal with media attention after her grandmother died, and Rylan was visited at the hotel by his celebrity friend Katie Price. Union J were stunned to find fans already gathered outside the Corinthia, handing them teddies and asking for kisses and autographs. Photos show the boys looking bewildered by all the fuss – was this how their lives would be from now on?

What's more, George found himself becoming the centre of attention when rumours paired him up romantically with fellow contestant Ella Henderson. 'The teenage sweethearts have been flirting for weeks and finally got together after being dared to kiss by their fellow contestants at their London hotel last week,' screamed a report in the *Sun*. 'Now they are inseparable and spend all their time holding hands or texting each other.' The *Daily Mail* followed with a headline claiming: 'Making sweet music: Union J's George Shelley and Ella Henderson in secret *X Factor* romance following their first kiss.' The media went all-out for this gorgeous new young couple, with countless features and news pieces speculating on how, why and when the two singers got together.

But was it the truth? In an *X Factor* video, Ella tried to lay the gossip to rest, but her shy giggling seemed to tell another story. She explained that, although she was single, she knew that people at home were beginning to think otherwise. The teenager insisted that she and George had simply found they had a similar outlook and had bonded quickly, becoming close friends. It wasn't anything more than that, according to Ella. Romance or not, the chemistry between the pair was there for all to see in the video packages broadcast to the nation, so the rumours weren't going to end there.

Still, the boys had each other to lean on. In the intense hothouse environment of the *X Factor* finals, with the boys spending every moment of every day together, they could easily have found that it was too hard – that they couldn't pull together after being a group for such a short time. But instead Union J bonded more tightly than ever and got to know each other's personalities. Asked to sum each other up in an interview in the TalkTalk lounge, JJ pronounced Jaymi 'bossy!', while Josh dubbed George 'cheeky'. George retaliated by calling Josh 'a womaniser' and Jaymi joked around, calling JJ 'a bit slow ... no, he's just never there!' Josh explained in a funny story that showcased how JJ could sometimes miss the point. Josh had been explaining that Triple J – as they then were – were unique because there weren't other three-piece boybands. Sweet JJ then chimed in that the boys were similar to the Sugababes – a three-piece girl group! The banter between the four of them was natural and playful – clearly this was a group of boys who'd become like brothers in the past few weeks.

Sharing bedrooms in the smart hotel had brought them even closer together – and up close and personal with each other's embarrassing secrets. JJ and Josh had to share a double bed in their swanky hotel room, but didn't want to get in each other's way accidentally, so they found a neat way around the problem – putting a pillow in between them. And the other boys had also discovered something funny about their bandmate Josh – his 'sleep-shouting'. After sharing a room with him one night, George got the shock of his life to see Josh sit upright in bed – fast asleep – and start chanting George's name. He was really weirded out – and even more so when it happened again. George didn't know what to do. Totally freaked out, he had to show someone else the strange sight of Josh's night-time ramblings, so he went outside to find a security guard. Of course, Josh was totally oblivious to this and all the other times he'd scared those around him at night. But George had more goss on his fellow bandmate, revealing that, rather than sleep-talk, Jaymi liked to sleep-sing! One night, he'd woken up George by warbling out the Jackson 5 classic tune 'I'll Be There'. The boys were certainly discovering each other's funny sides.

But when it came to Saturday night, all four members of the band had to pull together and set the fun and media spotlight to one side. It was their moment to put all their hard work into practice, and prove to the audience – and the judges, too – that they could be the boyband worth watching and voting for. Aptly, considering the romance rumours for George, it was Love and Heartbreak week. The show opened with all the finalists singing Gotye's 'Somebody That I Used to Know'. Union J were third up, but first they had to follow Jahmene Douglas and Christopher Maloney. With his sweet, soulful voice and confident stage presence belying his timid personality, Jahmene owned the stage with a mash-up of Amy Winehouse's 'Tears Dry on Their Own' and 'Ain't No Mountain High Enough' by Ashford & Simpson. It wowed the judges, with Louis proclaiming him a top *X Factor* star and Tulisa even claiming she wasn't able to find one criticism. Wild-card entry Christopher was up next, dazzling the judges with his version of the classic power ballad 'Alone' by Heart. He was winning the support of everyone for conquering his crippling stage nerves, with Nicole supporting his bravery and Tulisa appraising his strong voice. Despite their intense preparation, Union J would have their work cut out.

Their song choice was brave and contemporary – a mash-up of Leona Lewis's huge hit single 'Bleeding Love' and Nelly Furtado and James Morrison's duet 'Broken Strings'. It couldn't have been further from the Seventies rock of Queen the week before. Standing on a dark stage, with only dramatic shards of blue light illuminating them, the boys sang against a backdrop of bare trees, all dressed in boots, jeans and coats in muted colours. Their performance was in stark contrast to the 'let's have fun' atmosphere of the previous week's song, demonstrating that Union J were taking this performance incredibly seriously.

With his clear, strong voice, Jaymi confidently began to sing the first few lines of 2006 *X Factor* winner Leona's tune. Next, Josh took the tune and then all four joined in. Harmonising, moving together and singing their hearts out, Union J were beginning to take shape as a band to sit up and take notice of. As they began to sing 'Broken Strings', the boys strode forward, walking around the judges' table and into the audience. The studio crowd went wild, screaming and reaching out to touch their new heroes. As the song built to a crescendo, there was no doubt that this performance was at a totally different level to the previous week's. With their assured stage presence and tight harmonies, Union J had arrived. As they finished with a perfect harmony, the noise in the studio reached fever pitch. Surely they had proved themselves now – but what would the judges say?

Thankfully, Tulisa was straight in with the compliments – she could tell instantly they'd improved since their disappointing debut last week. She gave them a better judgement this week, praising their song choice, voices and fans! The looks of relief on Union J's faces as they realised their hard work had paid off for one judge, at least, were unmistakeable. The boys stood with their arms round each other, smiling, but the good news wasn't over. Gary was also delighted and impressed as he saw how the boys had turned it around. The boys laughed, thrilled, even as Gary again criticised Louis for his poor song selection the previous week. But they'd won him over tonight, and the boys couldn't have looked happier – this was going better than any of them could have expected. Would they be able to make it a full house of judges' approvals?

It was Nicole's turn to speak. Showing a side for comedy that the British public hadn't seen yet, she pretended she was preparing to deliver a crushing criticism, before coming in with a big compliment. The performance had worked a treat and she was impressed, too. That was it – they'd done it! With the screams and cheers from the audience reaching deafening levels, Union J embraced each other in unbridled joy at finally hearing what they could only have dreamed of. And Nicole wasn't finished with her praise, even making a prediction that the boys had the capacity to go on and sell out stadiums in the future! Josh was stunned and JJ pumped his fists in triumph.

Now it was Louis's turn to give his protégés the reward they'd been waiting for. He knew better than anyone how much effort the band had put in over the past seven days and felt deep down that they had an incredible, vibrant quality that the show needed. From the response of the studio audience, Louis, with his keen eye, believed they were destined for great things. After these amazing words, it was time for Union J to tell Dermot how this all made them feel. Surely it was fantastic after their drubbing last week?

It was. Josh was over the moon, but still looked overwhelmed by the reaction. They were all so chuffed to hear some positive words from the four judges. Over the high-pitched screams of the crowd, George tried to make himself heard as he vowed that they would continue honing their craft – but he was drowned out by the crowd's response. Dermot picked up on his popularity, joking that it didn't matter what George said – his fans loved him anyway. In good humour, he pointed out what was becoming blindingly clear – that Union J, and George in particular, already had incredibly passionate fans. George grinned and Jaymi laughed alongside him. The evening had been an absolute winner and now Union J could relax and enjoy the rest of the show.

And there were more amazing performances to come. Ella Henderson performed Minnie Riperton's ballad 'Loving You' and bowled everyone over with her stunning voice, hitting the high notes beautifully. Nicole gushed over the teenage protégée, and Louis predicted she could be set for the same success as huge stars like Adele. Whether or not she was dating George, Ella was turning out to be one of the most naturally talented stars of this series, deserving of special attention.

After losing her nan just a few days earlier, Lucy Spraggan fought through her grief to perform an innovative version of Kanye West's 'Gold Digger'. She especially impressed Gary Barlow, who'd tragically lost his baby daughter Poppy when she was stillborn just two months before. Bravely, Gary spoke out, referring to how difficult this terrible loss had been for him, and praising Lucy for doing the right thing in going onstage.

District 3 divided the judges with their version of the 1990s classic 'I Swear' by All-4-One. Gary was one of the harshest critics, aiming barbs at the band's musicality, which had up until then been their strength. Louis tried to defend his other group by shouting at Gary – although the Take That frontman sneaked in some positive words for his rival judge among the criticisms. He proclaimed that Union J had swept the boyband board that evening. Listening backstage, the boys must surely have taken some pride in this statement, despite feeling bad for their fellow group.

Rounding off the show, Jade Ellis took Amy Winehouse's heartbreak song 'Love Is a Losing Game' and made it her own, with Gary marvelling at how high the standard was this year – and it really was. MK1 got a disappointing reaction when they turned the Jackson 5's 'I Want You Back' into an urban number, with Nicole not being her usual effusive self and Gary damning them with faint praise. None of the judges thought their performance was going to set the world on fire. The mash-up theme continued with Kye Sones mixing songs by Rihanna, Eminem and Dido, but again, it didn't hit the mark with the judges. Clearly frustrated, Louis hadn't been gripped by Kye's below-par performance and his lack of engagement with the singer showed. Rylan Clark continued his march as the cheesy party act of the series, combining Deee-Lite's 'Groove Is in the Heart' with Psy's 'Gangnam Style'. Although she conceded it had been a silly number, hardly in keeping with the rest of the competition, Tulisa couldn't resist loving a bit of Rylan. After nearly managing to send him home last week, she'd clearly changed her tune. Predictably, Gary didn't agree with her – especially as Rylan had teased him by beginning his medley with a snippet of Take That's 'Back for Good'. After having his ability to hold a tune knocked by Gary, Rylan retorted with a deadpan joke that he had a car waiting outside for Gary – referring to Gary's dramatic exit the previous week. And finally, Melanie Masson belted out INXS's 'Never Tear Us Apart' – impressing Gary with her top-notch vocals.

It had been a mixed bag for the contestants in this early week. With their confident, atmospheric performance, Union J were definitely one of the victors of Week Two. But, of course, it wasn't over until the Sunday-night results show. Still, the boys enjoyed the break between performances by taking to Twitter to whip up support from their fans. Still wearing their outfits from the Saturday-night show, Union J snapped themselves holding up Twitter messages via their new Twitter handle @unionjworld to lucky fans. Looking sultry and gorgeous, Josh's message read: '@theshannonset We (Heart) Ya Shannon 🔝'. Sticking his tongue out cheekily at the camera, he held another message reading:

'@unionjsbabe LOVE YOUR PICTURE UJ xxx'. No doubt when they saw their messages the fans couldn't believe their idols were talking directly to them via the social networking site. JJ also joined in, holding a card which read: '@lukesbeanie Union J (Hearts) Ya!' and he teamed up with Josh to wish @curlynotfrizzythe1st a 'Belated Happy Birthday!' The messages showed the boys had a natural connection with their fans and they would only build on that relationship as time went on. But it wasn't all fun on that Saturday night – fellow singer James Arthur dramatically collapsed after his performance. Despite wowing the judges with his rendition of Mary J. Blige's 'No More Drama', James found that the pressure of *The X Factor* was getting to him and had a panic attack in front of the producers. Although an ambulance was called, he didn't go to hospital and soon recovered. The next morning, he released a statement, saying: 'I had an anxiety attack last night, maybe because I gave everything I had to my performance. I feel loads better this morning after a good night's sleep and I'm looking forward to tonight's show – there's no way I am missing it.'

Amid all the craziness, just a few hours later it was time for Union J and the other finalists to learn their fate. Tapping his legs nervously, Josh and the other Union J boys joined their fellow contestants onstage for what would become a tension-filled weekly ritual. Their survival was in the hands of the viewing public – would the judges' comments have helped boost their votes? It would be a travesty if they went home after such a sterling performance, but, as they'd already seen with Carolynne Poole's controversial eviction, on *The X Factor* nothing was guaranteed.

Back when it all began. Four fresh-faced stars in the making.

(Clockwise from top left): George Shelley, Josh Cuthbert, JJ Hamblett and Jaymi Hensley.

Four boys who quickly became the best of friends.

Larking around in London inbetween rehearsals and filming.
No good boy band is complete without a few onesies.

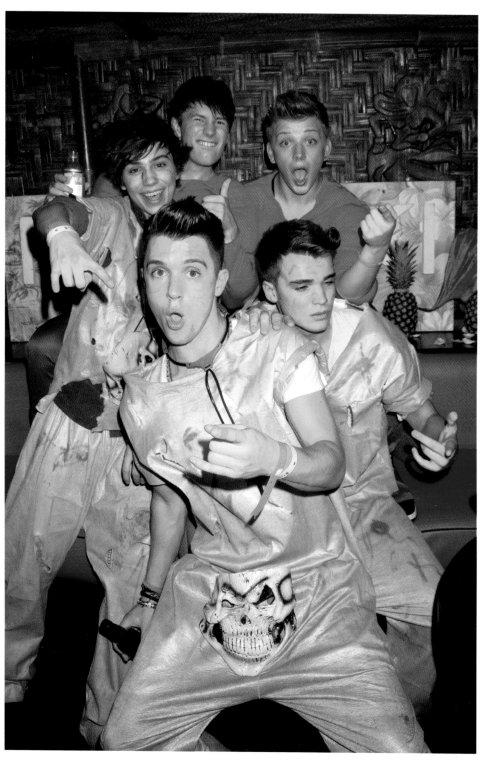

JJ, Josh and George getting into the party spirit, with District 3's Greg and Michael at Rylan's Halloween-themed birthday party.

On the way to the recording studio for mid-week rehearsals.

Outside the ITV studios, London.

Suited and booted for the *Skyfall* Royal World Premiere, the boys look relaxed and confident on the red carpet.

James Arthur was the first to go through, which must have come as a relief to the stressed-out singer. Lucy Spraggan's name was called next, followed by … Union J's name! The boys roared with joy, leaping up and pulling Louis into a bear hug. It was a huge relief for them, and thankfully the agony of waiting to hear their fate was soon over.

However, it wasn't all good news for the Groups. After District 3's underwhelming performance, they found themselves in the bottom two against Melanie Masson. Yet again, the judges found themselves in deadlock, so the results came down to the public vote. Luckily for District 3, they were saved and Melanie sent home – but it had been a close call. Union J may have had a triumphant weekend this time round, but their grit and determination would be tested to the limit over the coming weeks.

CHAPTER 6

UNION J FEVER: THE LIVE SHOWS, WEEK THREE

In Union J world, confidence was growing. After the incredible reaction to their *X Factor* performance in Week Two, the boys were starting to really enjoy their new lives. They'd had an incredible time onstage the previous week, and got the first, heady taste of that onstage buzz. The screams of the crowd had affected them deeply and they wanted more of it. It was clear that as a four-piece they had the potential to reach the top; and the mood in the band was high. Settled into their roles, their bond grew deeper as the weeks went by, which proved to be an invaluable support to them all, because by now, only a few weeks into the live shows, there was no doubt about it – Union J were famous.

If they were in any doubt about it, events that week would put those uncertainties to rest. Amid their hectic rehearsal schedule, the boys were booked to make an appearance at Brent Cross Shopping Centre in Hendon, Northwest London. Retail bosses and *X Factor* producers alike thought it would be a good way to build the *X Factor* fanbase and bring shoppers to the local mall. But they had wildly under-estimated the feverish interest already sparked by the boys – and the commitment of their fans. Keeping back news of where their appearance would be until the day itself, the boys at last tweeted excitedly: 'The info you have BEEN WAITING FOR! #MeetUnionJBrentCross shopping centre, London, TODAY at 6pm! Pass it on! Union J x.'

They couldn't have foreseen the chaos that ensued. Over the next few hours, thousands of fans poured into the shopping centre. Taking up all spare floor space, pressing against barriers and flooding in from buses and the car parks, they were all desperately keen to meet their idols. Holding up hastily written placards and banners that read 'We Love Union J!', the crowd of girls grew bigger and bigger. Soon the hashtag #MeetUnionJ was trending worldwide as word spread.

But it had spiralled out of control. Brent Cross security soon realised that the number of fans squashed into a small space was getting dangerous. If the boys were to actually appear, the ensuing hysteria could result in people getting injured. There was no way they could ensure the safety of all the young fans gathered in the shopping centre, and so they made the difficult decision to cancel the event. Looking forward to meeting more of their fans, Union J were about to leave for Brent Cross when they received the shocking news – they wouldn't be able to go. Realising that their fans – some of whom had been waiting for hours – would be bitterly disappointed, they quickly took to their Twitter feed to explain the situation: 'We are SO sorry, just about to leave BUT the security have told us we r not allowed 2 come as its a security risk. We feel awful. So sorry. X' They even took photos of them all holding up apologetic signs. 'We promise we'll make it up to you – sorry!' read Jaymi's, while Josh's said:'Josh is so sorry to everyone who turned up! Sorry sorry sorry. xxx' 'Sorry we couldn't make it tonight. JJ' and 'SORRY – it wasn't our fault! Love you. xxx' wrote JJ and George, as the four of them did their best to make amends.

Perhaps predictably, some fans became angry after feeling so let down. 'Waited 2 f**king hours for Union J to get to Brent Cross and they never turned up due to "a high amount of people". Such a waste of time,' read one angry tweet. The boys reacted to the negative tweets quickly, saying, 'To all u amazing people who turned up we are so overwhelmed for your support. It means the world. Tweet us a pic of u now and we will follow.' After an official statement released by *The X Factor* to explain the situation – 'Union J's "meet-and-greet" had to be cancelled as the huge number of people there meant it wasn't safe for them to appear' – the boys spent a worried few hours. This was supposed to have been a fun event to spread the Union J word and meet some fans. Instead it had turned into a disaster.

Luckily, they didn't need to fret for long. They headed out that night with some of the other contestants for a restorative dinner at hip Camden restaurant Gilgamesh. Arriving back at their hotel late at night, there were scores of fans waiting for them – the cancelled meet-and-greet at Brent Cross hadn't put them off. And the newspaper headlines the next day didn't blame the boys for the mishap. Instead, the *Daily Mail* heralded, 'They really ARE the new One Direction!' If ever there was a silver lining, this was it. Despite feeling awful for disappointing their fans, Union J realised that interest in them was growing by the day. And luckily, they had some new mentors in the pop industry to help them navigate this strange new world of fame – One Direction themselves. After meeting the global superstars backstage on the first week of live shows, the two groups had bonded, with George swapping phone numbers with the member he'd been most compared to – Harry Styles. With identical thick, curly brown hair, dimples and cute looks, the two heartthrobs found they had a lot in common. The *Sun* even reported that Harry had texted George a key piece of advice – 'Don't cut your curls!' And Union J were smart enough to see that being compared to the biggest band on the planet was a positive, not a negative. Josh in particular was really pleased to be spoken of in the same breath as One Direction, as they had been on the same *X Factor* path Union J now found themselves on. The boys wanted to look to the more experienced band as an example of what could be done – they would take the amazing success of One Direction and use it to propel themselves forward as far as they could.

Getting used to fame was a big challenge for the boys. After all, just a few weeks before they had been living normal lives and had been able to walk down the street unrecognised. Now, everything had changed. They had become public property – gossiped about in newspapers and on websites and followed on Twitter, with every word they uttered listened to by their fans. Sites were being launched by keen fans who dubbed themselves 'JCats', such as the Union J World News Tumblr site dedicated to the boys. It was a lot to take in at once. The photoshoots and interviews they'd given to the weekly magazines were also starting to hit the shelves – and everyone wanted to know how it felt to become famous. 'It's great,' George told *Star* magazine. 'It's crazy to think how we've gone from being normal to having fans following us everywhere.' Their lives were now incredibly surreal – the boys were experiencing the show from the inside after years of being viewers at home. They soon realised that being part of the *X Factor* madness meant they had no idea really how the public were reacting to them, and they couldn't equate their daily lives with now being famous to the nation. They simply couldn't see how it was possible. But still, one of the best things for the band was meeting their fans – although they were still getting used to that, too! Heading out on a shopping trip to Topshop's flagship store on London's Oxford Street, the boys got a sudden awakening as to how impossible it was now for them to walk around unrecognised. Nearly a hundred girls followed them around the store, passing the boys presents and notes scribbled with declarations of love. The boys were overwhelmed, and so happy to see that they'd already managed to connect with fans of the show.

Of course, the public wanted to know about the boys' romantic lives, too. Were they involved with anyone? Both JJ and Josh told *Star* magazine they were in the early stages of seeing someone from back home, whereas Jaymi confirmed that he was in a relationship of three and a half years. George used the opportunity to deny the Ella Henderson rumours on the record. 'I am single,' he stated. Even Louis Walsh teased the boys about the latest interest in who they were dating. He asked the boys which of them attracted the most girls – and the band knew the answer to that: an even split between Josh and George! The two gorgeous lads chuckled, abashed, as their bandmates teased them.

There was still plenty of time for fun, as Union J showed their fans in a Twitcam recording posted on the Friday before the show. Adorably all dressed in onesies, Jaymi showed off his joker nature by dancing on the bed behind his bandmates. 'Look, I'm a monkey today,' chuckled George, as the band started reading comments and shouting out to fans: 'Bless everyone who stands outside the hotel – we love you all so much!' Within minutes the whole band were doing silly moves to a chant of 'Pineapples, coconuts!' Their wacky humour was both endearing and entertaining.

But things weren't going so smoothly for the other *X Factor* contestants. After partying at London nightclub G-A-Y following the results show, Lucy Spraggan and Rylan Clark were reported to have caused 'havoc' in their plush five-star hotel. 'The group had been drinking heavily and could barely stand up as they left. When they arrived back at the hotel, Lucy had to carry Rylan up the stairs,' reported the *Daily Mail*. 'Not finished with the night's antics, he came back down and pulled his pants down in the street whilst making a lot of noise.' After allegedly throwing a floor sign at the hotel staff, the pair were asked to leave the Corinthia and so, on the Tuesday, moved into the less glamorous Hilton Hotel near the *X Factor* studios in Wembley.

Meanwhile, another contestant spoke up about a deeply traumatic childhood. Shyly spoken Jahmene Douglas revealed to the *Sun* newspaper the story of his harrowing upbringing at the hands of his abusive father. 'Every day I thought, "I'm going to die,"' he confessed, detailing how his father brutally attacked his mother for years, and how his brother eventually took his own life.

For Union J, with life getting so crazy and the attention focusing on the boys' personal lives and growing fanbase, it was a challenge to remember what was at the centre of this – the *X Factor* live shows. They had to try to keep focused on what mattered. In all seriousness, Louis knew that they could take it all the way, but it was still early days. He worried that getting so much adoration from the fans at this early stage would distract his group. Sitting down with the band to give them a serious talking to, he pointed out how far away from their dream they really were. Just because they had ardent fans already didn't mean that success was guaranteed. Plenty of groups in the past had not made it, despite having a good following, and he wanted them to heed his advice. Crucially, if they didn't get through each week, they risked their pop career being over before it had even properly begun.

George understood what was important and was focused on improving week on week. He wasn't afraid of some really hard work. And JJ agreed that getting some negative comments had actually helped them as a band – despite it being hurtful to be brought back down to earth with such a bump, it had made the band realise that they really needed to pull together and unite if they were going to make it on the show. The theme for the *X Factor* show that weekend was Club Classics, but as George explained, Union J were going to maintain their focus on how they sounded as a group. They had honed their singing so that it was as good as it could be and wanted to demonstrate their credentials to the viewers at home. JJ was looking forward to this opportunity to showcase their talents, but Jaymi knew that everything was at stake – and that just as quickly as it had been given to them, it could also be taken away. A lot of people had invested their faith in them.

Expectations were running high – not least from the boys themselves, who had promised the fans and the viewers that they would not let them down. The party atmosphere kicked off on the Saturday night with a bang, with a stunt-Dermot O'Leary performing flips and somersaults. This was to be a high-energy night – would the boys have what it takes? The remaining 11 finalists joined together onstage at the start of the evening to sing Chaka Khan's 'Ain't Nobody' before Union J had a tense wait to sing for their lives. They were halfway through the running order and had to sit through a number of popular acts.

First up was Christopher Maloney, who was fast proving that, despite not being a judges' favourite, he had the support of the viewers at home. He sang a disco version of pop duo Boy Meets Girl's 'Waiting for a Star to Fall' – and with his shiny suit and fake tan seemed more suited to a cruise ship than the *X Factor* live shows. The judges were beginning to realise that his angle was cheesy and naff, but Nicole still complimented Christopher on his perfomance. Tulisa didn't have that problem and really laid into the Scouse singer, accusing Gary of being hypocritical in slating Rylan when his own act, Christopher, was even more kitsch. After having a poor first two weeks, with two of his over-28 acts leaving, Gary was in no mood to lose another protégé. He urged Christopher to remember who put him in the finals – the voting public.

Union J's fellow group MK1 were next up, with a medley of 'Gypsy Woman (She's Homeless)' by Crystal Waters and

Tinie Tempah's 'Pass Out'. Gary and Tulisa were in agreement – the second half of their performance had been a let-down. Nicole, however, gave it high praise, even inventing her own term, 'shamazing'. Jahmene Douglas took on the soul styling of Aretha Franklin's 'Say a Little Prayer' and received a glowing reception from the impressed judges. Tulisa became even more impassioned, moving the shy singer close to tears with her emotional praise. Would Union J be able to achieve a similar impact with their performance? It remained to be seen.

First, they had to wait for two of the strongest singers in the competition to take the stage – Jade Ellis and James Arthur. Sadly, Jade was suffering with a bad throat, so her rendition of 'Free' by Ultra Nate was more muted than usual. It wasn't the dazzling performance everyone was expecting on the show, and Louis vocalised his doubts that Jade would be returning next week. James turned LMFAO's 'I'm Sexy and I Know It' into a heartfelt, acoustic track and won everyone over with his innovative musicality. For once, even Gary and Louis were on the same page, marvelling at James, who was definitely a different sort of singer to those that had often been found on the show.

From that high point, it was finally time for Union J to take to the stage. Dressed simply in white T-shirts, denim shirts and black jackets, the boys sat in a diamond formation. The screams began to build as Union J started singing – their song this week was Kelly Rowland's 'When Love Takes Over'. Josh and Jaymi sang the first few lines before all four boys began singing the chorus. They moved around the podiums in time, sitting in different positions, before stepping down onto the main stage for the crescendo. As fireworks rained down behind them, the crowd began chanting loudly, in unison, 'Union J! Union J!' It hadn't happened yet for any of the other acts – demonstrating without doubt that their fans were behind them 100 per cent after yet another sterling performance.

Tulisa, smiling from ear to ear, did her best to get her voice heard above the cheering audience. She congratulated herself for recognising that they were capable of so much more. And now, with the band improving all the time and gathering more and more fans, they were finally getting into their stride and were at the start of a great journey. Like the British public, who were now taking Union J to their hearts, the judges were aware that here was something special. Not just another boyband that might be over by Christmas, but potentially new superstars. Gary amazingly pronounced them the takers of the new boyband crown, as Union J hugged each other in amazement. He then warned them that their singing still required improvement, although he had been impressed. Once again, Union J had impressed Gary Barlow – singer-songwriter for one of Britain's biggest ever boybands – and they knew how hard-won that praise had been. They thanked him with genuine, humble delight on their faces.

Would Nicole be joining in with the chorus of approval? At the beginning of her speech, it seemed as if she did agree with them all, noting that Union J had a great onstage style. But, for her, there hadn't been enough vibrancy and she criticised the boys for slowing the song down when it should have been more in keeping with the week's theme, Club

Classics. As she attempted to carry on talking about harmony, Nicole was drowned out by the fans, still chanting their idols' names. As the boys tried to take it all on board, it was time for their mentor Louis to have his say. He wanted them to take the credit where credit was due – they'd put their all into the performance and the viewers at home were right behind this new band. Even Dermot, who was now onstage to talk to the boys, had to agree with Louis and supported Union J. He pointed out to Gary and Nicole that proceedings were still at a really early stage, so comparatively the band had done brilliantly. But Gary wasn't going to be won over that easily – he wanted to see tighter vocals from the four boys.

Dermot was quick to lighten the mood, which had become increasingly serious. Noting that the Union J performance had included an expensive firework shower, Dermot joked that the band obviously must have support. Jaymi laughed, and Josh grinned as he appraised the judges' comments. Yes, the band were pleased, but within reason. They accepted that they weren't quite there – at a boyband peak – yet. Leaving the stage to more shrieks and yells from the audience, Union J low-fived their fans, whose arms stretched out to get as close as they could to the band.

One by one, the other contestants showcased their songs for the week. Rylan Clark, perhaps predictably, went for another high-camp performance, mashing up Rihanna and Jennifer Lopez. Louis was now fully behind the out-there contestant, vowing to keep him in the competition. But Gary remained unconvinced and pointed out to Rylan that he was taking the spot of contestants who, in Gary's eyes, were more deserving of a place. Rylan's partner-in-crime, Lucy Spraggan, was up next, singing David Guetta's 'Titanium' and giving it another brilliant Lucy twist. The judges loved it and Tulisa even defended her mentee from the negative headlines about her social life. Playing the piano, Kye Sones knocked it out of the park with his rendition of Swedish House Mafia's 'Save the World' – moving Gary so much that he gave him a standing ovation. After a so-so week in the last show, Kye was back as a real contender.

Next up were District 3, who'd arguably been losing the boyband crown week on week to Union J. Would this be the moment they'd be able to snatch it back? They sang a Madcon/Chris Brown medley and upped their game with a tight, confident performance that wowed the judges. Gary was shocked at how the boys had managed to confound expectations and gave them huge praise. Nicole concurred, pointing out that the other groups had better not write District 3 off so quickly. The judges were unanimous; District 3 had proved themselves, and then some. Backstage, Union J must have worried. Only one boyband from each series had ever been remembered. Would District 3 be the chosen ones from Season Nine?

The show finished in epic style, as Ella Henderson gave a barnstorming performance of Candi Staton's classic 'You Got the Love'. Although the judges fell out over Ella's dance moves, they all agreed she was spectacular and more than deserving of her coveted place in the competition.

That Sunday, the remaining contestants stood stock still onstage, awaiting the results. For Union J, happiness was just around the corner, as they were the first band to be announced as safe and returning next week. They cried out in sheer unbridled happiness, hugging each other and jumping for joy. George put his head in his hands. He couldn't believe it – they were through! But there were still shocks in store. Despite his astonishing performance, Kye Sones found himself in the bottom two against MK1. Would the judges avoid deadlock and decide who they wanted to keep in the show that week? Predictably, Louis kept his protégés MK1 and Gary kept Kye. It was down to Tulisa and Nicole. Nicole decided to send home MK1, but Tulisa felt more of an affinity for MK1, as they reminded her of her first band, N-Dubz. Therefore, she sent Kye home. For the third week in a row it was indeed deadlock. The public vote would decide.

Dermot made the final announcement. MK1 would be leaving the competition. With one group down, only two remained. Union J had made it through again, but so had District 3. The seeds were sown for the Battle of the Boybands.

CHAPTER 7

HEADED DOWN? THE LIVE SHOWS, WEEK FOUR

Union J were on another high: they'd made it through yet another week of the show and, what's more, Gary Barlow had declared that they had a future as a group – and he didn't dish out praise like that to every act. With his years of experience at the helm of one of Britain's biggest pop bands, Gary knew more than anyone what could make a successful boyband, and what could leave one flailing. And interest from the fans was still growing. Hordes of chanting girls lined the streets outside the Corinthia hotel day and night, as well as outside the *X Factor* studios. The band always spent ages having their photos taken with them and signing autographs, showing the fans that they appreciated their support. George was even sent a fanbook, which a devoted crew of JCats had put together and sent on to their new favourite group in just a few weeks. George especially was amazed at all the work that had gone into making this sweet present – he was clearly touched by the gesture. Still, it was a bizarre life for Union J and one they could never have foreseen happening to them. They were enjoying every single bizarre moment of being in a famous boyband, and although it couldn't have been more of a contrast to their past lives, they welcomed every change that came.

Rehearsals kicked off with a bang on Monday. Following their usual meeting first thing with Louis, straight away the boys began dance rehearsals. This weekend's show would be the Halloween special, which was the boys' favourite party time, and they were determined to keep up the momentum that had propelled them into the pop stratosphere.

It wasn't all hard work, though. That week saw a huge treat in store for Union J. The latest James Bond film, *Skyfall*, had been the most hotly anticipated movie of 2012. Every celebrity worth their salt was dying to get a ticket to the world premiere, where the film's star, Daniel Craig, would walk the red carpet alongside fellow A-listers, royalty and Olympic stars. Luckily for the *X Factor* contestants, the event was happening during the series run, so on the Tuesday night they found themselves on their way to London's iconic Royal Albert Hall to face the world's flashbulbs. All the contestants had put on their glad rags and were ready for a night out, mixing with the A-list. JJ was on the edge of his seat with excitement, but before he left, he teamed up with George to squeeze in a quick filming session for their video diary. They showed viewers the room that Josh and JJ shared, showcasing the five-star luxury room the boys now called home. JJ cracked jokes to the camera as it panned around the dazzling interiors. He even showed his sweet side by holding up his cuddly toy monkey for everyone to see. The boys took the camera around the hotel and bantered with each other as George looked through JJ's phone to find the most embarrassing photo of him to show the fans.

But then it was time to get to the premiere. For Union J, looking super-stylish in their simple black suits, it was an incredible experience. 'This is amazing, just unreal! We just jumped out of our car and there were a million lights,' Jaymi told Absolute Radio, grinning delightedly at being at such a huge event. 'I'm a massive James Bond fan. *The X Factor* told us we were going to a premiere around this time, so we were all really hoping this was going to be it!' Even for George, experiencing the intense adoration of fans paled in comparison to being at the movie premiere the world had been waiting for. 'This is the most crazy thing that's ever happened to us! This is, like, more nerve-wracking than a Saturday-night show!' he laughed, as Jaymi joined in straight away. 'Yeah, this is worse than a Saturday night!' he said. 'I'm shaking.' After revealing that they were going to 'hunt down' Daniel Craig, the boys were asked outright who they thought their toughest competition was. 'Ella Henderson. She's just incredible,' said Jaymi, as George smiled shyly and giggled alongside him. 'She's like our little sister, she's got something really special.' Another interviewer wanted to know more and pressed Jaymi for further information. 'We just bonded straight away on the first week, us as a group and Ella,' he explained. 'Because she's so young and so talented, I sort of want to protect her a little bit.' Already the dad of the group, Jaymi's caring nature was evident as he talked about their friendship. 'She's always in our room, having a laugh,' he added, as George chimed in – 'In our onesies!' 'We believe in her so much, she's going to do so well,' finished Jaymi loyally. But there was one other big concern of the night – what should the Union J boys do if they met Prince Charles, who was also at the premiere? 'I rang my nan, who's a real royalist, and I was like, "What do you do if you meet the royal family?"' said Jaymi. 'She was like, "Just keep your mouth shut and smile!" and I was like, "OK, we'll do that then."'

It had been an amazing night for the boys but they were about to come down to earth again with a huge bump. The next day, the papers were full of glossy photos of Union J and other stars at the *Skyfall* premiere – but they also contained some bad news for the boys. '*X Factor* hopefuls Union J face being SUED by a pop manager who claims he put the band together,' read the report in the *Sun*. 'Julian White reckons Josh Cuthbert, Jamie 'JJ' Hamblett and Jaymi Hensley were part of Rewind, which he set up last year. But shortly after they began being noticed, White alleges they DUMPED him and went off with a new manager.' The article went on to detail the claims made by Julian White, who accused the three Union J members of breaking their contract and avowed: 'I'm coming after them for 5 per cent of their earnings.' Dramatic words – but friends of Union J hit back in the piece straight away. 'He managed them before George joined the group, so they're not even the same band as when he managed them,' the *Sun* quoted a source as saying. And Jaymi took to the band's Twitter feed that morning to refute the story. He tweeted: 'I do love it when sad people have to lie to hit the papers! #desperate! Jaymi. x' And the boys' manager, Blair Dreelan, added, 'Union J are confident that the ex-manager of Triple J has no contractual claims over the band.'

Following the headlines, the boys decided to put their worries to one side and instead get in the party mood –

again! That night saw Rylan Clark celebrate his twenty-fourth birthday. As would be expected from the flamboyant singer, he didn't go for a few quiet drinks and then to bed by 10pm. Instead, it was an all-out wild party – a Halloween-themed dress-up night at the Mahiki nightclub. One of London's most exclusive hangouts, it had played host to countless celebrities, including Prince William, Prince Harry, Rihanna and One Direction, but they probably hadn't witnessed anything quite like that night before. With the birthday boy dressed in a revealing American football outfit, all the *X Factor* stars joined in the fun and let their hair down in style. Lucy Spraggan turned up in a pumpkin outfit, while judges Tulisa and Nicole went for saucy, skimpy costumes that showed off their amazing figures. Union J got into the spirit of things, too, and wore surgeons' scrubs, dripping with fake blood. Despite this gruesome image, the boys still managed to look amazingly cute. The night soon descended into alcohol-fuelled debauchery, with Rylan and Lucy locking lips for the cameras. Yet again the next day's papers were full of 'Sprylan's' booze-fuelled antics.

There was almost no time to bring their feet back down to earth, as on the Thursday morning Union J met another of their pop idols – Robbie Williams. He was appearing on the show that week as a guest mentor and would be offering the contestants a masterclass. The Union J boys joked with the cameras as they went up to the seventh floor of the hotel to meet the legendary star. Robbie gave them his backing and good wishes for their success. First Gary, and now Robbie – Union J were on their way to getting a full house of support from the Take That crew!

After the exciting week they'd had, it was almost a relief when Saturday night arrived and the boys could get back to what they loved best – singing as part of a group. Things were already different this week, though, as Lucy Spraggan wouldn't be appearing. After being diagnosed with 'severe flu', she wasn't able to perform and had been given a free pass to progress to the next week's show.

Union J kicked off proceedings by starting the group performance of Usher's 'Without You', and they only had one song to wait before it would be their moment again. Kye Sones was up first and covered Robbie Williams's classic pop anthem 'Let Me Entertain You' – which was especially brave considering the man himself was on the show that night! Strutting around the stage, and even running into the audience, Kye cut a confident figure, which delighted the judges. Nicole was absolutely knocked for six and declared that her support was now behind Kye. But would Gary – Robbie's Take That bandmate – feel the same? He did, celebrating Kye's dramatic, confident stage presence and congratulating the singer on a barnstorming performance.

It was already time for Union J to head out onstage. Performing Beyoncé's 'Sweet Dreams', the performance began unusually with the boys sitting and standing on top of a black car. As was becoming their trademark, Jaymi began to sing first, and dramatic green visuals of a speedometer flashed around the stage behind them. This was a moody, Gothic version of the song, befitting the Halloween theme of the evening. Leaping off the car, the boys acknowledged the fans screaming their support by touching their hands as they walked across the stage. Giving it their all, they moved back to stand together as the song finished, out of breath and hoping that they'd once more convinced the judges of their worth. Tulisa was straight in with a positive comment, praising the boys' voices and singling out Jaymi especially, as his stunning vocals had shone that night. Looking flattered, Jaymi muttered his thanks. But it wasn't full-blown praise, as she criticised the boys for sticking to what they had done before – Tulisa felt they should have mixed it up a bit more. The boos from Union J's basecamp started to build, but Gary took his turn to speak – and agreed with Tulisa. Disappointingly, the Take That frontman also felt that Union J weren't pushing the envelope, or even their capabilities. He wanted to see more excitement, something he wasn't expecting. Would Union J be able to deliver again?

The boys nodded seriously. The expression on their faces was one of disappointment. As Jaymi bowed his head to the floor, they waited anxiously to hear what Nicole would say. Surprisingly, she had nothing but incredible words for the boys. Declaring their performance exceptional because of its stripped-back approach, her comments brought delight from the audience and thrilled hugs between Union J. For Nicole, she didn't need bells and whistles, just Union J, onstage, doing what they did to perfection. But Gary disagreed with her. Would this be another controversial judge's fallout? In his opinion, there had been too much technological input for the performance to retain the simplicity Nicole said it boasted. But she stuck by her words and commended the boys for listening each week to the judges' critiques. Thank goodness – they had managed to impress one judge at least.

Next up was Louis. Sadly, he wasn't giving his mentees unfettered praise like Nicole had done. He thought they hadn't quite reached the level they were capable of – and urged the viewers to support this group by picking up the phone. With Dermot now onstage, he came to the group's defence and again took Gary to task for his criticisms of the band's performance. Gary stuck by his words, insisting that he knew what was wrong with the band's musicality. With all the judges and presenters at loggerheads about the group, Josh spoke up to explain where the band had been heading that week. He earnestly explained that they had done their utmost to showcase their harmonies, as had been asked of them. Yet again, Union J were pleading their case to the viewing public, as well as to the judges, and vowing to work even harder. At the end of this touching plea, even Gary conceded they had done well overall. It had been a mixed bag for Union J, and now they had to wait and see how the rest of their rivals would do over the course of the evening.

Now a tabloid figure thanks to his antics with Lucy Spraggan, Rylan Clark decided to play on his notorious reputation with a darker-than-usual turn. Lowered onto stage via a large glass shelf, he moodily sang Britney Spears's 'Toxic' before mashing it up with Nineties dance track 'Horny' by Mousse T and Nicole Scherzinger's 'Poison'. Usually po-faced during these performances, even Gary giggled as Rylan mounted the judges' table. His confidence was irresistable and Louis was now Rylan's new big fan, complimenting him on his amazing stage presence. Tulisa – who'd been out on the town with Rylan at his birthday bash – cheekily referenced their night on the tiles with her comments, again drawing attention to Rylan's absolute command of the stage. He had the confidence of a much more experienced artist. Even Gary, hardly Rylan's biggest fan, was put in a good mood by the Essex lad's barnstorming performance. Joking that the singer had been drowned out by his loud backing track, Gary felt it was an improvement! As Nicole teased him, Gary conceded that out of Rylan's contributions to the show so far, this had been his best. What a turnaround: Rylan – arguably the contestant with the weakest singing voice – had won the judges over that week. Things were being turned on their head with these spooky goings-on on the Halloween show and Union J, watching backstage, could see they were far from safe.

With her hair teased into a dramatic bouffant and wearing a red silk cape, Ella Henderson delivered a haunting version of Evanescence's 'Bring Me To Life'. Gary was first to pronounce on Ella's increasingly obvious super-talent and claimed that she was running away with the number-one spot compared to her fellow contestants. However, Nicole wasn't so impressed, declaring it her 'least favourite' of Ella's performances. The former Pussycat Doll was concerned that Ella had sung it in the wrong register for her own particular voice. Tulisa loyally defended her mentee, praising her for bringing her own identity to these well-known songs. Still, Ella was clearly deflated by the muted reaction. Christopher Maloney delivered Eighties pomp and swagger with Cutting Crew's hit '(I Just) Died in Your Arms Tonight', but the judges' reactions made it evident that they all – apart from Gary – had tired of him remaining in the competition. Not only that, he'd garnered more negative press headlines that week for missing filming with Robbie Williams to go back up to Liverpool for a visit. The knives were out for Christopher now and Louis was going to deliver the harshest verdict. He declared that Christopher was not the star that *The X Factor* was aiming for. Rather, Christopher would be more suited to a career onstage in pantomime – ouch!

Next up was District 3. What would Union J's rival boyband bring to the table this week, when high drama and excitement was being demanded of all the acts? From the first glimpse of them in their white hooded tops and sharp suits (influenced by Stanley Kubrick's cult film *A Clockwork Orange*), standing out against a simple, stark background, they grabbed attention. Showcasing the close harmonies for which they were becoming celebrated, the three performed The Police's 'Every Breath You Take' mixed with Ne-Yo's 'Beautiful Monster'. They looked the part, but what would the judges say? Tulisa wasn't keen and Gary was even more disparaging. Slating the band for going backwards in their development rather than forwards, he couldn't find one redeeming feature. District 3 looked crushed as one by one they were picked apart by the judges.

What a week! So far the only acts to receive a positive reaction from all four judges had been Kye and, bizarrely, Rylan! Surely Jahmene Douglas, a judges' favourite thanks to his effortless soul voice, would redress the balance? Turning The Fugees' 'Killing Me Softly' into a sweet ballad certainly won over Louis, who anointed the humble vocalist as the strongest contender in the whole competition. Following such a spectacular performance, even Tulisa was unable to tell Jahmene that he'd done anything at all wrong, and Gary echoed her sentiments — it had been faultless. Finally, a triumphant achievement! Cool customer Jade Ellis looked the business in a sexy leather catsuit as she sang the Sugababes' 'Freak Like Me', but something about her attitude was lacking. She didn't seem to really want to be on the *X Factor* stage — and the judges had noticed. Nicole especially was shocked by the underwhelming impression Jade had left, and Louis worried what had happened to the spark that had won them all over at the audition stage. James Arthur brought the evening to an end with a deeply dark version of Eurythmics' 'Sweet Dreams'. It thrilled the judges and, for the first time, James was spoken of as a potential finalist.

It had been a strange evening for all the contestants — plenty of praise, but also plenty of criticism, too. And Union J had come in for their share of negative comments, which had knocked them for six. After such an exciting week, with parties, fan adulation and even a world premiere to dazzle the boys, they now faced an uncertain night's wait for the results show.

The words uttered by Dermot O'Leary the next night to indicate the results were about to be called struck fear into Union J's heart as they took their place onstage alongside the others. Who would be safe this week? Ella was first … followed by District 3! They looked disbelieving — after the drubbing they had received from the judges, they'd survived. Union J gave their fellow group a supportive hug as they left the stage. Did this mean good news or bad news for Union J? They'd have to wait to find out. Jahmene Douglas and James Arthur — the judges' favourites — were safe, too. So was Kye Sones, and — to his own elation, despite the boos from the crowd – Rylan Clark. Union J were sick with fear. Now there were only three acts left on the stage: themselves, Jade Ellis and Christopher Maloney. Would they squeak into the last safe space left?

But it wasn't to be, as Dermot called out the next name: it was Christopher! Boos and jeers filled the studio as the dreadful news sunk in. The Union J boys were now in the sing-off and they would have to pull something extraordinary out of the bag to ensure they weren't out of the competition. Like all the other bottom-two acts, they had to sing a different song from the one they'd performed earlier. They'd chosen the rawly powerful 'Perfect' by Pink and the boys' expressions as they sang their hearts out showed they were still in shock. The performance was heartfelt and emotional. George looked on the verge of tears. No one could be in any doubt that all four were desperate to stay in *The X Factor*, and they pulled each other into a group embrace as the song finished.

Would Jade be able to demonstrate the same poignancy? Singing a stripped-back version of Dido's 'White Flag', emotion and grit was written all over her face, affecting her performance. Off to the side of the stage, Josh comforted an upset JJ, hugging his bandmate close. Jaymi and George looked despondent. What was in store for them? Could this really be the end?

It was time to find out. Josh put his arms around JJ and George, while Jaymi closed his eyes as they waited to hear what the judges would say. Would there even be another deadlock, for the fourth week running? First up was Louis and his voice cracked as he vowed to stand by his act. Predictably, he supported Union J, sending home Jade, but he was still close to tears. It was Tulisa's turn next – Jade's mentor. Again, the result was a shoo-in, with Tulisa backing her own act and ditching Union J. Dermot noted that, so far, the judges' votes had been easy to call – but the next two verdicts would be the real decision makers.

And he was right. Both Gary and Nicole had had positive things to say about Union J before – Nicole more than most. Would they stand by the boys? Nicole looked surprised to be asked her verdict first. She considered the merits of both the acts: Jade, with her feisty personality, who had battled through many hardships and, when on form, had one of the most unique and cool voices out there. Then she turned to the boys. Jaymi's lip quivered as he and his bandmates waited to hear what her thoughts were. It was good news for Union J – Nicole felt that they'd applied themselves more and shown a dedication to improving that she'd noticed. Thankfully, their hard work had won her attention. More boos rose up in the crowd as Jade's audience support rallied.

The decision lay with Gary. Union J's hearts raced and they struggled to catch their breath in these, the tensest few minutes of their life as a group so far. He admitted that, as someone who'd been through the boyband experience himself, he had been extra-tough on the young upstarts and knew they were capable of so much more. Despite this, Gary declared, he knew there was something special in the fledgling group and he wanted to see just how far they could go with this early potential. Would these be the sentiments that saved Union J? Gary went on, complimenting Jade's undoubted vocal skill, but debating the issue that had dominated over the course of the night – did Jade really have the hunger to succeed that would mark her out as an *X Factor* winner? As Jade shook her head, Gary delivered Union J's fate in a few short words – he was sending Jade home.

It was the words they had been waiting for – Union J were saved. They'd peered into the abyss and survived, thanks mainly to the hard work and positive attitude that they'd displayed so far. But as they pulled into a tight group hug, while the audience whooped in delight, they knew how close it had been. They left the stage shaken and trembling with adrenalin, but happy: they had lived to fight another week.

CHAPTER 8

BACK ON TOP:
THE LIVE SHOWS, WEEK FIVE

J osh looked resolute as he stood with the rest of the band in their rehearsal studio, talking about the devastating experience they'd undergone on Sunday night. Union J were filming a video diary and were under no illusions that they'd dodged a bullet at the weekend. Despite everything, they were determined not to be brought down by the negativity of landing in the bottom two; they would instead use the experience to spur them on. JJ knew that they were competing against some truly exceptional acts and George concurred – there was no such thing as a safe spot in this year's competition, no matter how many fans they had. Jaymi,tucked up cosily in his monochrome onesie, knew that things were just going to get harder the further into the competition they got and the fewer acts that remained. The boys were feeling serious, thankful to be there and ready to redouble their efforts to stay in the show. In a Twitcam session they made on the Monday night to speak to the fans, it was clear they were feeling vulnerable about what had happened. 'What do you reckon went wrong on Saturday night?' Josh asked their Twitter fans. 'Because we were really heartbroken. Let us know what you think we can do to improve.' 'Being in the bottom two was the hardest thing I've ever done,' declared Jaymi. 'We just want to know what it was we did wrong,' pleaded George. After that bruising experience, the boys were feeling raw – and desperate to know how they could make things better.

They might have made it through to Week Five of the live shows, but if anyone thought that was the end of the Week Four drama, they were mistaken. Feisty Jade Ellis wasn't going to go quietly, and following her eviction she spoke out angrily to the press, putting the boot into Union J in the process. 'I don't think the decision on Sunday was based entirely on the sing-off. The judges were thinking about their own acts,' she told the *Sun*. 'People have said my performance was better than Union J's, but Tulisa was out there on her own when she chose to put me through. The vote could have been tactical. Maybe the judges thought Union J were less of a threat to their singers in the competition.' Harsh words indeed, but it was another reminder to Union J of how much they needed to prove themselves. There were still large swathes of the public who weren't convinced they deserved a place in the competition when other talented singers were leaving each week.

Union J faced a curious contradiction. There was no doubt that they had a huge following, with devoted JCats following their every move and screaming their names wherever they went. The boys loved meeting their fans every day as they waited in the freezing winter cold to chat to and get autographs from their idols outside their hotel. Some particularly determined girls had even managed to get into the smart Corinthia hotel, necessitating more security to be put around the group. 'Fans have broken into the hotel twice now. One of the times they were right outside our rooms in the corridor,' a stunned Josh told the *Sun*. 'We could see them trying to work out which rooms we were in before someone noticed and they were removed by two beefy security lads. Since then our security has been at least five or six times tighter.' George was amazed at the lengths to which the fans would go to get close to the boys, after discovering that the hotel bar had been deluged with applications for jobs from fans. He still felt like a regular guy and this leap into showbiz still felt totally bizarre.

But as Sunday night had demonstrated, this fervent fanbase didn't translate into Union J being one of the more popular acts on the show. The very fact that they had been in the bottom two meant they had some of the fewest votes of everyone. Speaking to their video-diary camera, George begged all the fans who spent time supporting and following the band to translate their devotion into votes. They knew how close they'd come to losing their big chance, and Jaymi agreed with his bandmate, giving the camera a cheesy grin as he canvassed for votes as well.

Outside of Union J's world, more negative headlines swirled around the *X Factor* circus. Show boss Simon Cowell's friend, Eighties pop star Sinitta, claimed that 'next year will be the last' for the contest, and after triumphing over the BBC's rival show, *Strictly Come Dancing*, for a number of years, ratings that year were down. Viewers had averaged at around 8.4 million for that weekend's show, with *Strictly* getting 9.6 million. With this hoopla going on, it was more important than ever for Union J to stay focused on the task at hand. If they allowed themselves to become distracted by the tabloid feeding frenzy around them, there was every chance they'd lose confidence and self-belief.

Thankfully, it seemed that going through these tough obstacles had only served to strengthen the group. For Union J, it was a case of what didn't kill them made them stronger. At this halfway stage in the competition, the boys' bond had actually become stronger. As they learned more about each other's personalities and went through more ups and downs together, they were able to support and boost each other more and more. Their roles were becoming set – Jaymi, the oldest and most articulate, took on more of a dad role, whereas George, the baby of the group, was like their little brother. But although they had fallen into different roles within the group, they all pulled together to work just as hard as each other. Within Union J there was no weak link and their ambition to succeed only grew stronger. After his experience in other groups, Josh especially knew that fierce application of their efforts was the only way they could ensure that they stayed in the competition. If the viewers at home could see how hard they were working, then hopefully that would garner more support for the group.

Monday morning after the drama of Sunday night saw them regroup with Louis Walsh. He had been stunned by the disappointing results the night before, and knew how hard it had hit the boys. The relationship with their mentor was as important to Union J as ever. Asked by a journalist whether they 'blamed Louis' for landing in the bottom two, the boys were vociferous in their loyalty. 'Never, ever!' stated Jaymi. 'Last week's song choice was ours – Louis let us have free rein. He's there to mentor us, not to manage us, and he gives us incredible support. He's the fifth member of Union J!' 'Lovely guy,' agreed Josh. Louis's tactic this week was to ensure that Union J's natural personalities came across – they weren't a cookie-cutter boyband; each had a distinctive personality, which needed to shine. Coming so close to the end had really rammed home what they could have lost out on, and Jaymi, keenly aware that this was a once-in-a-lifetime opportunity, was determined to make it last.

The will to make it big came across in the celebrity magazines, too – where demand for an interview with *The X Factor*'s hottest guys increased as time went on. *Heat* magazine boasted an 'exclusive' that week with Union J. In it, the boys were once more asked about the comparisons to fellow *X Factor* boyband One Direction, and whether they thought they'd be able to follow in their footsteps. 'I'm not sure it's possible to be any bigger than One Direction, but that would be amazing – that would be the dream,' said Josh. 'If we can be half as successful as One Direction, we'll be chuffed.' But it was also important to try to draw a distinction, otherwise Union J risked being seen as copycats. 'We're just different,' Josh went on. 'They're very young-poppy. We're a bit like a young Maroon 5.' It was a tricky line for the lads to walk – on the one hand they were grateful to be spoken of in the same breath as such huge stars, but on the other they didn't want to lose their own developing identity.

As the week went on, there was no time to rest, despite the boys suffering winter bugs. The weeks of intense hard work, adrenalin and long days were taking their toll. All of the boys had come down with nasty coughs and colds, as they explained to that week's video diary. The gruelling regime had wiped the boys out, but they couldn't let their illnesses take them over. Despite feeling below par, the boys had busy evenings to fit into their diaries, too. Monday night saw them attend the annual Pride of Britain Awards, where top celebrities awarded accolades to deserving members of the public. The entire *X Factor* family shared the red carpet with royalty – yet again – as well as Prime Minister David Cameron and stars such as Holly Willoughby, Alan Carr, Carol Vorderman and Spice Girls Emma Bunton and Mel C. For the boys, this was an incredible blessing, and watching the moving stories of ordinary people doing extraordinary acts of bravery really affected them. But it proved an uplifting experience, and Josh drew positivity from being around so many great examples of kindness. But for George, the excitement of the evening was encapsulated in the stars they were now rubbing alongside. They met venerable actor Sir Ian McKellen, who George knew best as Gandalf from the *Lord of the Rings* movies – and it made his night.

Just a couple of nights later, it was time for Union J to attend another awards do – *Cosmopolitan* magazine's Ultimate Women of the Year Awards. There, the atmosphere was much lighter and fun-filled, and the pre-show interviews allowed them to have a laugh and let their hair down. Asked what impresses the guys, Josh grinned. 'Smiles, honestly, smiles,' he said, with George adding in cheekily, 'And have a twinkle in the eye!' 'Be yourself, don't worry about being someone you're not,' said Jaymi, meaningfully. 'Be honest, be who you are – that's all that anyone looks for.'

Throughout all the showbiz razzmatazz and illness, Union J poured their hearts into daily rehearsals for Saturday night's show. The theme that week was Number Ones, and after the downer that had been the previous weekend, the boys were determined to make this something to really enjoy. 'We're going to go back to basics, back to the feel we had at Judges' Houses,' said Jaymi at the *Cosmopolitan* Awards. 'Just back to being four mates that love to sing, not worried about all the production, just be us.' 'I think this song we're doing on Saturday isn't the kind of song we'd usually pick,' explained JJ. 'But it's just going to show our fun side.' 'Have some fun and relax a bit,' added Josh, looking as if he couldn't wait to get onstage and release some of the pent-up tension. 'We've been given another lifeline by the judges, so we've got to go out this week and prove to the judges why we need to be in this competition.' 'Really let loose,' laughed Jaymi.

While Union J were running through their routine and song for the last time just a few hours ahead of Saturday night's show, dramatic news arrived. Lucy Spraggan was quitting *The X Factor*. After missing the show the previous week due to illness, the talented singer hadn't made a proper recovery and faced missing another week of the competition. She'd not been able to rehearse her planned performance of Rihanna's 'Umbrella', and fears were growing as to whether she would be able to take to the stage for the live show. After the public backlash against her 'free pass' the previous weekend, Lucy made the decision to pull out of the competition for good. 'I am gutted not to be able to continue on this journey, but I'm not well enough to perform,' she said in an official statement. 'To accept another free pass, having missed last weekend, would not be fair on the others in the competition. I wish them all well. I would like to express my thanks to everyone who has supported me. There is no way that this setback will prevent me from fulfilling my ambition.' Shock rumbled through the remaining *X Factor* contestants as they came to terms with the news. Rylan Clark – with whom Lucy had closely bonded (the pair dubbed themselves 'Sprylan') – was especially devastated that his show BFF was leaving. 'Gonna miss u being with me so much @lspraggan I love you, x' he tweeted.

But the show had to go on. The Union J boys had promised fun in that week's performance, and going by the relaxed, cheeky attitude they displayed in the week's VT, that was what they were going to deliver. The boys bantered for the cameras as they teased each other about the different 'roles' they'd adopted in the band – Jaymi as the de facto parent of the group and Josh being the band comic. After teaming up with their fellow contestants for an upbeat, infectious version of Carly Rae Jepsen & Owl City's party anthem 'Good Times', they didn't have long to wait. Yet again Union J would appear at the start of the show and only Rylan was performing before it would be their turn. Even by Rylan's standards, this week amped up the camp levels to 'through the roof' as he performed Madonna's 'Hung Up' mashed with its inspiration, ABBA's 'Gimme! Gimme! Gimme!'. Strutting around the stage like a peacock, with bright-red feather epaulettes, Rylan gave a shout-out to his crocked partner-in-crime, dedicating his song to Lucy Spraggan. Rylan's big supporter on the judge's panel, Tulisa, began proceedings by congratulating him in her best *TOWIE* voice.

She summed up the change in fortunes Rylan had undergone: people now appreciated his stage skills and charisma, and he was a worthy *X Factor* finalist. Even Gary saw fit to praise Rylan's vocals that week, despite claiming that this could be his last week in the competition. Nicole wasn't having any of his negativity and instead gave Rylan a rave review.

The Essex singer's popularity wasn't in doubt, but now it was time for Union J to see if theirs was still up to scratch. In front of a backdrop of CGI rain effects, Josh and George strode onstage to begin singing Taylor Swift's 'Love Story'. It was the first time George was showing off his guitar skills in the live shows and he strummed confidently as Josh took the first few lines of the hit song. Walking on from the side entrances, Jaymi and JJ harmonised with their bandmates as the four of them grouped together onstage. Looking relaxed, Union J playfully showed off the best of their musical ability as they belted out the romantic mid-tempo number. As the song finished to cheers and whoops, the boys gave nervous smiles. But had they done enough?

It certainly felt like it at first, as Tulisa's initial comments were about the clever song choice. She could hardly be heard over the audience's screams. Louis basked in pride as Tulisa continued to stress how important the track choice had been in finding what would work for Union J and what wouldn't. In her opinion, 'Love Story' had been spot on, as the girls who loved Union J would want to see them singing a romantic tune to their fans. She was over the moon with their performance and her previous doubts about the band's potential had been laid to rest. As far as Tulisa was concerned, choosing the 'fun' option had worked in Union J's favour. Now it was Gary's turn to speak – and first off, he had some words of warning for them, explaining that after Sunday night's decision to send Jade home, Gary had worried that he'd called it wrong. Before Union J had a moment to digest this comment, Gary turned it on its head – their sterling work this evening had convinced him that he had backed the right horse. But like every week, Gary didn't deliver 100 per cent acclaim, noting that George needed to improve the way his voice melded with the other bandmates'.

Wreathed in relieved smiles, Union J looked at each other – this was going fantastically well so far. Nicole put the focus back onto George's musical talent and hailed him for playing his guitar onstage. Her words were all positive, although they lacked the dramatic passion of Tulisa's praise earlier – but, overall, she was pleased to see what the boys were doing with their talent. Only Louis was left to complete the praise, and of course he was as effusive as ever. Joking that they didn't just have a new attitude, they also had new haircuts, Louis yet again delivered his traditional verdict on his group – they were set for the same kind of international success as the world's biggest boy groups. From the stage, Dermot quizzed Gary on what he meant when he critiqued George's singing. Gary retorted with a quick-fire jest about George's hair, but explained that it was all about the boys making their voices sound effortlessly connected. They were a group, so when singing together each voice needed to feel blended with the other.

Dermot asked the boys for their reaction after such a great reception from the judges – it had all been good. A contented-looking Josh agreed with the host. It was such a great turnaround after the week before, and they could only hope that the judges' verdicts would translate into viewer votes. The band had done their utmost, and now they hoped to reap the rewards. The atmosphere was lighter, looser as the boys stood onstage – and Dermot obviously felt it, too, as he quizzed JJ about his past as a jockey, joking that he must have competed as a child, before complimenting him on his 'David Essex' image with the white shirt and waistcoat. Things felt fun. The boys had delivered on their promise. Now it was up to the viewers to decide.

Kye Sones was up next, and after his impressive Robbie Williams rendition of the previous week he took on another pop classic – the New Radicals' 'You Get What You Give' – with a high-octane performance that saw him run around the stage right up to the judges' table. But something didn't quite work, as Nicole made clear in her halting verdict. Nicole seemed unsure what she felt about Kye's over-the-top performance, and Tulisa also damned him with faint praise. Next came James Arthur, and after being encouraged to showcase his more urban side, he did so in a version of No Doubt's 'Don't Speak' – inserting a new rap segment into the heartbreak song. It could have gone horribly wrong, but talented James kept it fresh and inspiring. All the judges praised his courage and confidence – Gary especially was dazzled by the edgy singer and his unpredictable musicality.

Ella Henderson sang a stunning, stripped-back and sloweddown version of Katy Perry's 'Firework'. It certainly won over an emotional Nicole, who gushed that she felt she was inside a film and had begun seeing dramatic lights! Mixing it up again by coming on from the side of the studio, District 3 entered into the party spirit, too, with an energetic version of Taio Cruz's 'Dynamite'. But it didn't convince the judges. Tulisa looked pained as she explained that she'd found it naff and embarrassing – the boys had overshot their capabilities. Louis shouted his discord with Tulisa's opinion over the boos, but to no avail. Gary was on Tulisa's side that week, agreeing that the boys had departed from where their strengths lay as a vocal harmony group. They were trying too hard to be something they weren't.

After that demolishing of Union J's rival boyband, Jahmene Douglas accomplished another amazing performance – this week taking on Beyoncé's 'Listen'. Louis was so enthused by his spectacular showcase, he assured Jahmene that his future wouldn't include returning to his supermarket job. The judges were staggered by his outstanding talent – which couldn't be said for Christopher Maloney, who rounded off the night. With his melodramatic version of 'All By Myself', he awaited the judges' reception, shaking and welling up. Nicole complimented his efforts in delivering a difficult song, but Louis was less kind. Again, he knocked Christopher for being an old-fashioned singer, and Tulisa also had words of warning for the Liverpudlian vocalist.

The judges' favourites had become clear: Ella Henderson, Jahmene Douglas and James Arthur. In their own, different ways, they saw Rylan and Christopher as not deserving of a place. Union J, District 3 and Kye Sones were somewhere in the middle, and the boys knew that a boost in public support was vital to keep them safe that week. The tension mounted, but the next night, the first act through was announced, and it was Union J! Over the moon that their hard work had paid off, the boys left the stage. Following them was Jahmene, Ella and James. Christopher also won a place in the next round, despite boos from the audience. Now it was between Kye, District 3 and Rylan for the last final place … and it went to District 3.

Singing for survival, Rylan brought out the big emotional guns, delivering a haunting rendition of Des'ree's 'Kissing You'. Kye sang Jason Mraz's 'I Won't Give Up' and brought the audience to their feet. Nicole was first to choose and naturally supported her act, Rylan, hailing him for bringing an emotional component into the competition. And, of course, Gary – hardly Rylan's biggest fan – backed his own act, Kye, who Gary believed had the best voice by far.' Yet again, it was down to these judges who didn't have an act in the sing-off. Which way would Louis go? Although he'd praised Rylan in the past, he decided to go with vocal talent and also supported Kye. It was time for Tulisa to call it, and her loyalties had now changed. Despite trying to send Rylan home at the beginning of the competition, she had become a huge fan and enjoyed his crazy performances each week. She made her decision and saved Rylan. Brought to deadlock once more, the public had the decision. Who would prove most popular with the viewers at home? It was going to be Rylan – so Kye had to leave the show.

Another *X Factor* shock had been delivered, leaving Gary Barlow with just one act left in the competition. Backstage, Union J celebrated at making it through another week, but their rollercoaster ride was far from over.

CHAPTER 9

THE BOYBANDS' BATTLE: THE LIVE SHOWS, WEEK SIX

Monday morning saw business as usual for Union J, which was now far from their previous life of slogging away at office jobs and uni classes. Instead, clutching coffees and snacks, with George carrying his guitar, the boys were confronted by an army of JCats and paparazzi, who gathered to meet them as they made their way to rehearsals. Despite the surreal nature of their lives now, they were getting used to it and were grateful to have survived another week in the *X Factor* bubble. In a cheery mood, George wrote on their Twitter page: 'Good morning everyone! Just want to say thank you and give a massive monkey hug to everyone who picked up the phone this weekend!' 'Still over the moon in getting down to the final 7 in the comp,' added JJ. 'Thanks sooo much peeps, you are all amazing for your support.' 'So glad we are still in the competition! I couldn't imagine waking up on a Monday morning and not heading to rehearsals! So thank you :D,' wrote Josh. Louis, too, wanted to give his band the credit they deserved for making it through. As they arrived for their weekly catch-up, Louis praised them for their professionalism and for showcasing the best of their abilities. They were getting better and better each week.

The boys' growing confidence as pop stars was evident from their first official Union J video diary, which they made that week 'for a bit of fun' and posted on their YouTube account. Taking the fans backstage at the rehearsal studios, it demonstrated beyond doubt that Union J were having a ball, showing them at rehearsals, filming for *The Xtra Factor* and having breakfast and lunch in the canteen. Jaymi and JJ even filmed a little comedy segment, taking it in turns to plait a girl's hair! (JJ, the ex-jockey, teasing that he'd done this regularly on horses' hair!) They even gave fans a little taster of what was in store for Saturday night's show, as the boys practised their version of Coldplay's 'Fix You' – their beautiful melodies blending with George's guitar playing. They finished off the VT with a hilarious segment seeing the boys 'escape' to supermarket ASDA in Wembley with fellow contestant Rylan (who had just been allowed to return to the Corinthia hotel, after being turfed out previously with Lucy Spraggan). To the confusion of fellow shoppers, the boys ran around the store, with Josh clutching a bunch of flowers. Who could they be for? The boys weren't telling.

At this stage in the competition, the remaining seven *X Factor* contestants were, incredibly, only a month away from the Final. The chance of each of them winning the competition was getting higher and higher each week – and so, certain provisions had to be made. Each of the remaining finalists had to do a photoshoot for the winner's single, meaning that if they did triumph in the Final on 8 December, production of their new song could hit the ground running. Josh explained that, although he felt their chances weren't the highest, they'd enjoyed the process of shooting the front cover for the winner's single, and it had made them realise that this dream wasn't totally out of their grasp. JJ agreed, pointing out that it was only a short time before the winner would be crowned. Josh turned on the dark gallows humour, joking that there were only six people he needed to finish off to grab victory!

As the *X Factor* Final grew ever closer, more focus was being placed on the remaining contestants – and any finalist who was considered unworthy of their place was feeling the heat. The backlash against Christopher Maloney cranked up a gear. Just a couple of weeks ago, booted-off MK1 had accused the Liverpool singer of being the 'biggest diva', and now it was Kye Sones's turn. Speaking to the *Sun*, Kye said: 'All of us have got really close, and then you've got Chris. We've been a really strong group and he's been an outsider – and that's nothing to do with any of us lot. He's very tactical. There are two different people – one when cameras are there and one when they're not there. Everyone is the same person off and on camera, apart from Chris – and that's why it's frustrating for all the contestants.' With nothing but compliments for the rest of his fellow contestants, it was becoming evident that Christopher's attitude was increasingly riling his *X Factor* family. Somewhat wisely, Union J kept their opinions on Christopher to themselves. Still in the competition, they knew that any fallout could have a dramatic impact on their standing. Rumours were also swirling that Christopher was coming top of the phone votes each week – allegedly panicking *X Factor* boss Simon Cowell, who was far away from the action working on the American version of the show.

There was nothing Union J could do about the growing controversy, so instead they kept their heads down, rehearsing like crazy and continuing to enjoy the new opportunities offered to them. One of these was a top celebrity party: the launch of Kim and Kourtney Kardashian's new clothing range for high-street store Dorothy Perkins. The boys rocked up late to the launch on the Thursday night at super-smart London restaurant Aqua – after their photoshoot for the winner's single held them back. Arriving at the same time as Kim Kardashian herself, Union J understood that to many of the guests there, they were still unknowns, and so they waited for superstar Kim to move along the red carpet first. 'We were like, no, we'll stay behind. We didn't want to do the walk and everyone think, "Who are them four?"' said Jaymi to ThisisMax.net. 'We're over the moon to be here – we think we're just four normal lads, and the next thing you know we're at Kim Kardashian's party!' added JJ.

How they were dealing with the sudden fame was something that everyone wanted to know about. Now many people knew who they were, how were the boys coping? 'It's mental – I suppose each event we go to, we get a bit more used to it,' explained Josh. 'But I don't think we'll ever get used to it – people taking photos of us and you guys interviewing us!' 'I'm usually the one out there taking photos, wandering around Leicester Square!' pointed out Jaymi. The boys were then asked another question – which Kardashian sister did they fancy? JJ chose Kim, Josh Khloe and George Kourtney. Jaymi dealt with the question well – choosing Khloe because she'd 'come out of her shell' the last few weeks on *The X Factor USA*.

Union J fans certainly had their pick of online interviews with the boys that week, as they also took to the backstage lounge on *The X Factor* to answer some questions from the fans. Josh revealed that his ultimate song to sing on the show would be rock'n'roll classic 'Great Balls of Fire', and that his favourite programme was *Deal or No Deal* – with him tuning in as regularly as he could. And teasing his growing band of female followers (with his model looks, Josh was now fast becoming the heartthrob of the group), he confessed that he would rather kiss Louis than a chicken. With his deadpan jokes about the difficulties of kissing a chicken's beak, fans loved seeing their idol's funny, sweet side. Jaymi and George also teamed up to answer Twitter questions in a separate video, and bounced their witty sense of humour off each other. When he claimed that he'd take his mobile phone on a desert island to save himself, George pointed out that he wouldn't be able to keep it charged. As the boys bantered, Jaymi was asked who he would take on the desert island with him. It was clear the singer wanted to avoid direct questions about his personal life. Claiming he wasn't sure who he would take with him, George came to his rescue, explaining it would be him, as they were currently sat close by. And what would George take with him? Naturally, it was something sweet and quirky – a cloud, to provide him with water. Jaymi put his head in his hands, mock-affectionately, as George delivered another witty riposte – he would take Josh with him as he was the only member of Union J strong enough to kill an animal for food. Giggling away, the boys were enjoying this release from the hard work they'd been putting in.

Certainly, by this stage, the boys were becoming known for their quirks. Jaymi, the leader and organiser; JJ, the sweet daydreamer and Josh, the ladies' man. George, without a doubt, was the smiler – his happy-go-lucky nature had been noticed by all. 'Does he ever frown?' laughed the interviewer to the other Union J boys at the Kardashians' party. 'Have you seen the Tweets when you're on the show? Everyone's talking about your smile, constantly!' 'He actually goes to sleep smiling,' revealed JJ. The One Direction comparisons weren't going away, either. But after so many weeks, the boys now knew the best way of dealing with it. 'It's amazing to think that maybe one day we could be like them, but we don't want to be them,' said Jaymi. 'We really want to find our own stamp and I think that's something we'll only find when we come out of the competition. We're a new band, so every week we're trying to do something that other artists have years to develop.' His perspective on what they were able to achieve at this early stage in their life as a band was impressively wise – and boded well for Union J's future, too.

For George, the focus returned to his love life. If he thought he had the chance of privacy while the *X Factor* circus was still going on, he was much mistaken. Grainy tabloid photos of him and Ella taken on the Thursday night of that week appeared in Saturday's papers. Showing the two teenagers holding hands, it appeared to confirm their romance, which both had been keen to dismiss as just a close friendship. '*X Factor* couple finally go public on relationship,' the *Sun* headline read, with a photo showing George and Ella walking through London's West End. 'Ella and George are the sweetest couple,' the paper quoted a source as saying. 'It's so lovely to see them together now they're not denying it. They are thrilled they've both got far enough to get on the tour. It means they can spend more time together next year.' But the supposed lovebirds weren't confirming any rumours. George insisted yet again that they just had a friendship – and that all of Union J felt like her brothers.

The theme of Saturday night's show was Best of British, and for Union J this marked a particularly important connection. Tying in with Remembrance Sunday that weekend, George dedicated their performance to the armed forces, as his older brother Will was currently serving as a Royal Marine Commando in Plymouth, after going out to Afghanistan to fight three times. And the armed forces connections didn't stop there: many members of Jaymi's family had served in the RAF. And Josh's dad had been in the Navy for 15 years. The boys were incredibly proud of what their families had achieved in the name of supporting their country, and although their career paths had taken them down a different road, they wanted to do what they could to show them how much they appreciated what they'd done.

Fans who had watched their video diary already knew that the boys would be singing Coldplay's 'Fix You', but in the backstage interview George explained that they felt ready to show a more vulnerable, moving side to their performance, which tied in with the week's theme. After the devastating impact of being in the bottom two a fortnight ago, Union J hoped that this affecting song would keep them in the competition – but they weren't counting their chickens just yet. In no way did they feel they were immune from being in the bottom two once again, and having been there before, their nerves were in shreds each Sunday evening. And this Sunday would be no different, explained JJ – things were going to get more traumatic, not easier, as the Final loomed ever closer.

Wearing their Remembrance Day poppies with pride, they joined in with the other finalists for a stirring version of 'Beautiful Day' by U2. This Saturday night, more focus than ever would be placed on the contestants. There was no room any more for makeweight acts, and certainly during this joint performance Union J's charisma and confidence was obvious for all to see.

Perhaps sensing that his controversy would bring more viewers to the show – even if they didn't like him – the producers put Christopher Maloney up first. And it can hardly have been a coincidence that he chose Elton John's 'I'm Still Standing' as his Best of British tune that week. It was a sharp, spiky performance – the singer knew he was battling a rise in public negativity towards him. Instead of delivering her normal enthusiastic verdict, Nicole looked deadly serious this week as she tore apart Christopher's central problem – he always sounded cheesy. The judges' frustration with the unpopular contestant was palpable – everyone had had enough. Tulisa was visibly fed up and hardly had the energy to tear into the singer, instead spelling out her opinion that he wasn't a relevant artist for today's pop market, despite having an inarguably good voice.

Things picked up with another amazing performance from Jahmene Douglas as he tackled Robbie Williams's classic ballad 'Angels', giving it the intense emotional punch he was becoming known for. Louis, in delight, decided that with this performance, Jahmene had secured his place in the competition's Final. Tulisa used the opportunity to praise Jahmene while backhandedly criticising Christopher at the same time – pointing out that he had managed to take an old song from the 1990s and make it relevant for the current times. And Gary concurred, noting that 'Angels' had been sung countless times before by many different singers, but nothing had ever come close to Jahmene's interpretation. He was really impressed. Next to appear were District 3. After their mauling at the hands of the judges last week, would they be able to pull it back by singing Eric Clapton's 'Tears In Heaven'? In stark contrast to the all-party atmosphere of the previous Saturday, the boys kept it simple, with just a piano and stools as their only props. All smiles, Tulisa was definitely in support of what the boys had done, crediting Louis for a good song choice and returning the vocal harmony group to what they did best.

It seemed as if they had pulled it off – but before they could breathe sighs of relief, Gary had some harsh words for them. Despite their good efforts on the song that night, he had big doubts that District 3 were the future of boybands. It was a vague criticism, not picking out their singing or style, but still just as devastating – especially as he compared them unfavourably in this respect with Union J, who Gary felt did have this potential. Bad news for District 3, but an amazing seal of approval for Union J. It was the first time Gary had publicly stated that he preferred them out of the two boybands – and his comments would serve to help them later on that weekend.

She'd said she had something unexpected in store for Saturday night and Ella Henderson wasn't joking. Instead of one of the big torch songs she had become known for pulling off in style, Ella went for Tinie Tempah's 'Written in the Stars'. Gary was incredibly pleased with what she had achieved by taking on such a different style of song and believed Ella had secured her place in next week's show. Nicole also assembled behind Team Ella, highlighting the fact that, at this stage, she was the only remaining girl and was acquitting herself brilliantly well. Even Louis delivered a terrific compliment, comparing Ella favourably to the 2006 winner Leona Lewis.

Then it was Rylan Clark's turn. Like Christopher, he was an outsider at this point in the competition, but he was hugely popular with his fellow contestants. He always brought out-there fun to his performances and this week was no different. Singing a Spice Girls medley, Rylan kicked off in style, filming a skydive and bringing the judges – apart from Gary – to their feet, dancing. Predictably, Louis absolutely adored what Rylan had done with the pop classics, and the screams were at a deafening pitch as everyone cheered the star on. Tulisa was also on side with her fellow judge, feeling that Rylan's high-octane performance had showcased exactly why she brought him through to the next round last week. And even Gary was willing to pay him a compliment – Rylan had delivered an upbeat, enjoyable number that even he had liked watching.

After such a high, it would be hard for the next act to follow. And, as an extra challenge for them, it was Union J's turn. They hoped that this song would be a great demonstration of their musical talents and that the emotion would resonate with the audience as well. Bringing the tempo down for their stripped-back vocals on Coldplay's 'Fix You', the boys delivered an incredibly powerful, tear-jerking performance. Jaymi's vocals in particular were at their most impressive, soaring above the music. As they put their arms around each other at the song's climax, all four boys looked emotionally wrung-out. They had given it their all, but would that be enough?

Speaking first, Tulisa was once again impressed with Louis that night, who she believed had chosen great songs for his two remaining acts. Displaying amazing foresight, however, the feisty Londoner believed that this also created a problem – with both boybands doing so well, this pitched them directly against each other, so fans of boybands would have to choose between one or the other, giving them far fewer votes than the other contestants.

Gary had more words of advice to offer them about their musicality – he still didn't think they had managed to nail the blend of their vocals, which he'd criticised them for last week. Still, his overall feeling remained positive, and he backed Union J for bigger things to come. Nicole was especially impressed by their dedication that week, and for their consideration in citing the good work done by the armed forces as the inspiration for their performance. For Nicole, the highlight of the number had been Jaymi's voice. It truly had been exceptional, and she noticed his amazing talent in singing solo, in tune and in total control. Louis was full of praise for his boys, but urged the viewers at home not to become complacent. When it came to the crunch, the boys needed votes like never before in order to fully explore their potential in the competition. He also had special praise for Jaymi. Louis understood what Jaymi had been through in his years of thwarted ambition and disappointments in his music career, and just how important this was to him. Union J and their mentor had a supportive relationship – something Jaymi would need more than ever in the coming week.

As Dermot joined the boys onstage, he noted that the boys had received some terrific comments that week. Josh agreed, but again pointed out that they wanted the opportunity to take things even further. But was there a sense of rivalry with District 3? Josh conceded that, as they were the only two boybands remaining, it was natural that they'd be compared with each other. But this wasn't what Union J felt themselves – District 3 were no more a rival than all the others still remaining.

Only one more act had to take the stage – James Arthur. Putting his own edgy spin on Adele's 'Hometown Glory', he had all the judges behind him. For Tulisa, James's involvement in *The X Factor* was the culmination of her dearly hoped-for wish that the programme could showcase some more unusual artists who drew on more urban roots. With James, Tulisa had found that act.

Before long, it was once again time to find out who would be through to the following week. On Sunday night, the remaining seven contestants lined up to hear Dermot – hopefully – call their names. The first act through was James, followed by … Rylan! With his mouth open in complete shock, the fans' favourite shook his hands in glee and hugged his mentor, Nicole. Despite his popularity, it was a huge

Stars in the making: the boys ooze charm when they appear at the
Cosmopolitan Ultimate Women Awards, October 2012.

Rumours that George was dating fellow contestant Ella Henderson turned out to be false, but their friendship was clear for everyone to see.

Boys' nights out:

Top left: Josh and 2012 winner James Arthur pulling faces as they're snapped on their way to the Prince's Trust comedy gala.

Top right: JJ papped outside celebrity hangout Mahiki.

Bottom: George on his way home from Mahiki.

All smiles as the boys travel around London.

Top: Performing live at the X Factor TalkTalk secret gig.
Bottom: Arriving for the Live Finals in Manchester.

The real journey begins as the boys embark on The X Factor 2013 Live Tour. They're rocking the stage here at the Manchester Arena (*top*) and the Motorpoint Arena, Cardiff (*bottom*).

Union J join in with Red Nose Day, accepting Jessie J's challenge of eating worms and crickets. *Bottom:* Arriving at the BBC Radio 1 studios to record Radio 1's Red Nose Day Challenge with Nick Grimshaw.

Union J have been together less than a year,
but they're already stars – and the future looks
very bright.

shock to see him go through. George chewed his fingers nervously, while viewers could make out Josh pleading under his breath for their names to be read out. Jahmene's name was called next – making Nicole the only judge to see her three acts progress through to Week Seven. Who would be next? It was Ella, undoubtedly a deserving recipient of a place in the following week's show.

The three acts left onstage were Union J, District 3 and Christopher Maloney. Whatever happened, Louis was bound to be disappointed as at least one of his boybands would end up in the sing-off. But he could take hope from the fact that, if Christopher landed in the bottom two, the judges would be sure to vote him off. The last safe place was going to … no, Dermot wasn't going to reveal the names until after an ad break. The tension in the studio was at breaking point. Minutes passed like hours as Union J waited for the show to come back on air. Finally, Dermot stepped onto the stage and announced that the last safe place in Week Seven would be going to … unbelievably, Christopher.

Gasps heard around the studio quickly turned to boos as the Scouse singer jumped for joy. Union J and District 3 were utterly crestfallen. And now they would have to sing their hearts out – again – to try to save their skins in the competition. It would be an echo of that time at Bootcamp, months ago, when Triple J had gone up against GMD3. That time, they had lost out to the other boyband. Was history about to repeat itself?

First up were District 3 with 'Just the Way You Are' by Bruno Mars. Nerves clearly got the better of them, as their harmonies and notes were all over the place. Waiting at the side of the stage, JJ had his arm around Dermot – in just a few minutes it would be their turn. Standing together onstage, it was all Union J could do to conquer their crippling nerves. Would the boys be able to prove that they were deserving of a place in next week's show?

Their survival song was Adele's 'Set Fire to the Rain'. Giving it their all, Union J sang powerfully and with obvious passion. Again, Jaymi was the star of the vocals, delivering such raw energy it took your breath away. Sitting behind the judges' table watching the second of his acts sing, Louis looked heartbroken, Whatever happened, he would lose tonight. With their breathing jagged, adrenalin coursing through their veins, Union J took their place alongside Dermot and District 3 to hear who would be saved. Controversially, Dermot asked Louis – the mentor for both bands – to deliver his verdict first.

Things kicked off big time, as Louis dug his heels in. He wasn't willing to call it and declare support for one of his acts over the other. Vehemently, Louis gave up his vote and said that he would leave it to the other three judges. As Union J applauded their mentor, Dermot pressed him for a decision – did he really want to abstain from the voting process? Louis wouldn't budge. He would not choose one act over the other. That left the three remaining judges to rule a majority between them. With an odd number left, there was no chance it would go to deadlock. Union J would have to hope that at least two out of the three judges were behind them.

The vote went to Gary next. Before delivering his verdict, he explained his thinking. He had previously gone with District 3, who he believed had the stronger voices. His words shocked Union J after his positive comments of the night before. But, despite this, Gary wasn't so sure about District 3 now, as their performance in the sing-off had been wildly below par. And in addition to that, the hunger and determination of Union J shone strong. Gary made his decision — he was sending District 3 home and saving Union J.

Josh swallowed nervously as Dermot moved on to Nicole. Would she put her vote behind them? Again, she began by complimenting District 3 on their strong vocal stylings — their harmonies were normally so tight and impressive compared with everyone else. Jaymi held his hand over his mouth – the emotion was getting on top of him. But Nicole had made her mind up based on what she felt inside and what was becoming increasingly evident to all the judges — that Union J were putting everything they owned, and then some, into the competition. She decided to send home District 3, sealing Union J's fate.

As the *X Factor* music kicked in, Union J took a few seconds to realise what had just happened. They had been saved! Jaymi put his hand over his heart, and all seven lads onstage joined in on a group hug. It was touching to see the affection between them when they had just been pitched so competitively against each other. Although Tulisa's vote wouldn't count that week, Dermot asked who she would have gone with. Sadly, it hadn't been a clear sweep that night, as she would have saved District 3 over Union J. But it didn't matter – Union J had survived after another traumatic week. Now they were the last boyband standing.

CHAPTER 10

OUT AND PROUD: THE LIVE SHOWS, WEEK SEVEN

That week, a Twitter message arrived for Jaymi that would change his life forever. A teenage fan had caught wind of the rumours that were bubbling online claiming that Jaymi was gay. He'd messaged his *X Factor* idol directly to ask if the stories were true as he was gay himself and wished that Jaymi could be out, because he didn't have anyone to look up to and was finding it hard to fit in and tell his parents.

The tweet went straight to Jaymi's heart. He hadn't deliberately been hiding his sexuality, but nor had he directly addressed it since becoming famous. In actual fact, Jaymi was gay and had been out to his family and friends since he was 14. He'd begun to feel differently to those around him and in a moment of clarity speaking to a friend, he had realised what this meant. 'I'd always got on better with girls, and loved doing the girly stuff and hanging out with them,' he told BBC Radio 1Xtra in a documentary of 2013. 'Then, when I was 14, one of my friends went to Sylvia Young in London and he was talking about someone who was gay, and I was like, oh my God, that's what it is!' Upon realising his true nature, Jaymi decided he wasn't going to keep his sexuality a secret and instead bravely decided to come out. Although his family was loving and close, he didn't know how everyone would react. Would they accept him as he was?

Happily for Jaymi, telling his family that he was gay at a young age didn't create any problems at all – they loved and accepted him just as much as before. It gave him a positive attitude towards his sexuality and his life. 'I came out when I was 14 to my family and friends and never had one piece of negativity,' he told the *Sun*. 'Because I came out when I was young, my family have had time to deal with it – they've been amazing,' he explained to BBC Radio 1Xtra. 'They had time to realise that it's not going to be as easy as: right, I get a girl pregnant, you get grandkids – we're going to have a talk about how we're going to do it! I think families just want you to be happy and I think you need to seize it. It's the best thing I ever, ever did.'

Jaymi had also found happiness in recent years with his boyfriend Olly. They'd met in a bar where Olly worked, and romantic Jaymi fell straight away for the gorgeous blond with the big smile and dimples. He knew he'd have to ask for his phone number. 'He strolled in like a little charmer and won me over!' Olly wrote on Twitter when a fan later asked how they'd got together. Previously, Jaymi told *Bliss* magazine, he'd just 'jumped into relationships', but he knew that this one was different. This was despite an embarrassing start when, during the first week of going out, Olly walked straight into a wall in Jaymi's flat, knocking himself uncon-scious. The couple bonded so quickly that all their friends gave them a relationship name – Jolly!

Jaymi knew what he had with Olly was special, and so in 2010 he took him on holiday to the beautiful city of Rome, where he proposed. The boys knew that an engagement meant their relationship was solid – something Jaymi was relying on even more now his life had taken a crazy turn with Union J and *The X Factor*. 'He's really good at listening,' Jaymi told *Heat* magazine about Olly. Their families were thrilled to hear that the boys were engaged, and their wedding is rumoured to be happening later on in 2013.

He had never wanted to hide his sexuality, or his relationship with Olly, so Jaymi had been debating when to come out with the news. He knew that *The X Factor* was happy for him to go public, too. After all, many of that year's contestants – Lucy Spraggan, Jade Ellis and Rylan Clark – were gay and out. This tweet gave him the confidence and the inspiration – maybe now was the time. He sought advice from their mentor, Louis. The two had an honest chat where Louis reassured Jaymi that he would be fine and should be open about it. 'Put it this way, both of my big boybands had a gay member in them,' Louis told Jaymi, referring to the late Stephen Gately of Boyzone and Mark Feehily in Westlife. 'Do it.' Enormously reassured, Jaymi and Louis worked out what to do – he would give an interview to a national newspaper that weekend. The boys already knew that Jaymi was gay and were chuffed that he'd decided to come out properly to the public.

But for the moment Jaymi had to put his plans to the back of his mind, as he and the rest of the boys came to terms with what had happened on Sunday night. They'd made it through another week – but only just. They had been utterly crushed to find themselves once more in the bottom two, but being saved by the judges had been an incredible boost. Yet again, they'd been on a rollercoaster of emotions. And one special person in particular had found that her heart was in her mouth waiting to see what would happen to Union J on Sunday's show – Ella Henderson. Waiting for the boys in the green room backstage, Ella was in floods of tears as she rushed up to her 'big brothers' and hugged them when they made it through. As George and Ella embraced backstage, it was clear they had a deep connection – romance or no romance. In an interview with *Fabulous* magazine out that week, Ella again tried to quash the rumours, saying she and George were simply 'in sync' with each other.

Monday morning saw Union J attend their usual debrief with Louis and he conceded that they'd been through the mill. In the evening that had been dubbed the 'battle of the boybands', the four boys had gone through a traumatic time. Union J looked exhausted and devastated as they considered what had brought them so close to the end. More than anything, Josh wanted to avoid this terrible fate again – it had happened to them too many times. Louis stressed that the only way to ensure success was down to yet more hard work. They were now within touching distance of the Final and were the winners of the group category; being the last band standing, they had every chance of making it. There was no time to feel sorry for themselves; Union J would have to put the shock to one side and concentrate on their next performance.

But there wasn't enough time just yet to digest all the drama of Sunday night and focus on preparing for the coming weekend. Louis – and all the other mentors – had a surprise in store for their hardworking protégés. Monday afternoon saw the remaining *X Factor* contestants arrive at London's St Pancras station, wheelie suitcases in hand. They were off to board the Eurostar train and head for EuroDisney, which Josh revealed that morning on their Twitter feed. 'Going somewhere SO exciting today!!!!! Ahhhhajakahakabs thank goodness we are still here!! Josh, x' he wrote, adding. 'WE ARE OFF TO DISNEYLAND PARIS!!!!!! Ahhhhhh … soooo exciting!! I can't wait to go on the flying Dumbo ride!! #UnionJDisneyLandParis Josh. x' To celebrate the theme park's 20th anniversary, the remaining six acts had been invited to take part in a spectacular event. Dressed in cosy winter woolies, Ella joined the Union J boys as they arrived at the station in high spirits, playing around for the cameras and posing up a storm in their Mickey Mouse ears.

Hearing the news that they were to be given this amazing treat was a real boon to the boys. Arriving at the park, they got stuck into having some serious fun with their *X Factor* family. George and JJ braved the high-speed rollercoaster, with George still smiling throughout the ride while JJ screamed. For George, after going through such a horrible experience on Sunday night, being able to enjoy himself was the release he needed. And it was a funny experience, too − George and JJ sat next to each other on the rides and George giggled away while JJ hollered and yelled non-stop. Buddies Rylan Clark and James Arthur walked around the park carrying Mickey Mouse balloons, while sweet Jahmene Douglas shopped for a present for his mum. Ella joined Josh, JJ and Jaymi again for more hair-raising rides − always accompanied by a burly minder from the show. But it wasn't all fun and games − that night, they were scheduled to perform at

EuroDisney's special 20th anniversary concert in front of thousands of fans. Louis hoped that this opportunity to perform in front of fans would serve as a confidence-booster Union J and get them into great shape for the weekend's forthcoming show. Disaster nearly befell Union J on their away day, too, as George felt unwell after going on too many rides. He ended up asleep in bed, missing all the fun of the afternoon, which saw the remaining three Union J lads plus Jahmene win in a tug-of-war contest against Christopher Maloney, Rylan and James! Despite having great fun, the boys were concerned that George wouldn't recover in time for the evening's show. Luckily, and just in the nick of time, the teenage singer felt well enough to join his bandmates onstage.

That evening was a big deal for the boys. They were performing alongside their fellow *X Factor* finalists to a rapturous crowd of 2,000 fans – their biggest gig yet. In front of a festive, atmospheric *Sleeping Beauty* castle, the boys sang Leona Lewis's 'Bleeding Love', which went down a storm with the fans, who were screaming and filming their idols on cameraphones for posterity. It was their first gig outside of the *X Factor* studios and the boys did themselves proud. Tying in with the theme of the show that week – Guilty Pleasures – Union J had indulged their childish side with a trip to the ultimate theme park and, as Louis had hoped, having the opportunity to perform outside the show made them realise how much their fans loved them. Jaymi mused on the journey the boys had taken in such a short time – after all, only a few months ago, they had been Triple J, rejected from *The X Factor*. Now look at them! The trip had done them good

– giving them a break from the gruelling routine of *X Factor* life and demonstrating that they had what it takes to survive outside the Season Nine bubble.

But they were still in the thick of the hoopla, and their growing popularity was in no doubt as the boys continued to give countless interviews to the media. Magazine features hit shelves by the bucketload, with fans desperate to snap up any little tidbit on the boys. Speaking to *Bliss* magazine, the bandmates bantered as they showed how close they'd become in a relatively short time. 'George helped the dynamic of the group, as before it would be two against one if there was an argument,' explained Jaymi. 'But now we're like brothers, and Jaymi's our mum,' added Josh. 'I'm not the mum! Maybe the dad,' laughed Jaymi. And JJ confirmed that Josh was the one with an eye for the girls: 'Josh loves the ladies, he's the womaniser,' he revealed. They were always willing to get into the spirit of things, too, answering silly questions and 'fessing up to pranking JJ. 'We creep into his room while he's asleep, film him snoring and then wake him up with loads of noise so that he jumps!' said Jaymi.

Their devoted JCats were behind them all the way as they continued through to Week Seven, but it had hardly been the smoothest of journeys. Now Union J's mums decided to speak out and try to rally the voters to keep their sons' dreams alive. 'We need people to vote for them, they're just not getting enough,' Josh's mum Kathryn Browne told the *Sun*. 'Chris Maloney is running away with the votes. Maybe the fans think Union J might be safe and don't bother calling.' The bizarre Christopher situation rumbled on in the papers that week. Finding himself hugely popular with the phone votes, he had become 'public enemy number one' with the *X Factor* crew after repeatedly turning up late for rehearsals. According to a report in the *Mirror*, the Liverpudlian was left 'close to tears' after being subjected to a blasting from the producers. 'Contestant timekeeping is important to ensure that production runs smoothly and Christopher was spoken to by producers after arriving late for rehearsals on more than one occasion. The matter was quickly resolved,' an *X Factor* spokesperson told the MailOnline.

Union J tried to focus on the massive task ahead – a superb performance that would ensure they escaped the dreaded bottom two again. Rehearsals became even more intense than before. 'We're coming back fighting this week,' Josh told *Heatworld*. 'We've put so much more work into this week already, so fingers crossed we won't be in the bottom two. It's now getting to the business end of the competition where it's really hotting up and the talent is amazing, so we've got to try and get on the same page as Jahmene, Ella, James and Rylan.' As a break from the pressure, the boys had another glam night out planned for that week – the premiere of *The Twilight Saga: Breaking Dawn – Part 2*. After attending the *Skyfall* premiere, the boys knew what to expect from such a glitzy celebrity event and dressed super-stylishly in black suits with velvet jackets. But *Twilight* superfan Jaymi couldn't pretend that he wasn't incredibly overexcited. 'I'm massively obsessed with *Twilight*, so every time I look around I'm, like – ooh!' he told Sugarscape.com. 'I'm such a fan, it's unreal!' His bubbly glee at being at the premiere was adorable, as he fangirled like crazy every time a star of the movie walked the red carpet.

They would have thought it was impossible, but the weekend brought even more eventful happenings into Union J's world. Jaymi sat down with Leigh Holmwood of the *Sun on Sunday* to give his coming-out interview. It would appear in the next day's newspaper – and then there would be no going back. But there was no time to fret about the impact – the boys had to get ready for the show. For the very first time, they would be opening, so after all coming together to sing Tulisa's 'Young' as the group song, it was their turn. Wearing directional grey suits and standing on a plinth, Josh took the first few lines of Carly Rae Jepsen's huge hit 'Call Me Maybe', the song they'd previously showcased at Judges' Houses. Would it be their lucky charm once again? For a change, George then sung the next few solo lines and soon the whole group were singing together, performing impressive harmonies. The boys then jumped off the plinth and got the whole crowd going with handclaps for the last few bars – the party atmosphere was set. As Union J hugged each other at the end of another impressive performance, the studio audience went wild.

Tulisa began to speak – but had to shout to be heard over the roars of the audience. Unfortunately, she didn't have many positive words, beginning with a criticism of the song itself, which she didn't like. Although she attempted to look beyond that, her overall verdict was that they hadn't managed to achieve the whole point of the theme: putting an edgy twist on a cheesy song. Her comments went down badly with the fans in the audience, while Union J nodded, hoping the next judge would have something more positive to say. It was Gary, who was smiling from ear to ear – he loved it and disagreed entirely with Tulisa. Hearing his words, Josh gave a thrilled thumbs-up. Gary was all about Union J this week, believing that now they were out from the shadows of the fellow groups, they really had been able to shine. But despite this, they had to ensure that they didn't lose focus – and the boys understood that.

Although Nicole, up next, delivered some praise in her opening comments, she was clearly bothered by something else. And it was the fact that Union J kept jumping off plinths at some point during their performance – she was getting fed up with seeing the same thing. Jaymi laughed, recognising that this was becoming Union J's stage trademark, as they had done it many times before. Nicole explained her stance: she didn't expect the band to transform their stage routines into over-the-top choreography, just to put in more creative effort and produce something new. At this point in the competition, it wasn't just enough to bang out some amazing vocals – the whole stage experience had to be exceptional, too. After complimenting his band, Louis delivered his increasingly familiar refrain – urging the viewers at home to vote for the boys. He was clearly worried that they would wind up at risk once again.

Dermot was keen to focus on that key issue, directing his question to their mentor. With all the fans that Union J evidently had, screaming the boys' names around the studio, he was confused as to why the popular group were having trouble with the phone votes at home. He wanted to know what Louis thought the reasons for this were. In typical Louis style, he avoided directly answering the question, instead proclaiming again that Union J could be the success of the future. It was down to George to try to put his finger on why Union J were having a tough time with the votes. Unsure of what to say, George offered the opinion that it might have been down to having two boybands on the show – something that Tulisa had flagged up the week before. George shrugged, looking to Josh for support and vowing yet again that they were always willing to work hard.

The boys' 'little sister' – Ella Henderson – was next, turning the *Grease* classic 'You're the One That I Want' into a slow, heartfelt ballad. It was an unusual choice, but Ella crushed it with her amazing voice and stage presence, and Gary congratulated her on another sterling delivery, which he thought was her best. Nicole concurred, as she was always moved when Ella took to the stage. Yet again, Ella had dazzled the judges with her exceptional talent. James Arthur also turned another pop standard on its head – transforming Frankie Valli's 'Can't Take My Eyes Off You' into a guitar-led track. Although Louis was unconvinced that the track was the best choice in the world, he was impressed again with how James had treated it. And Gary was about to make an incredible pronouncement – he was backing James to win! It was another sideswipe at Christopher Maloney – even his own mentor didn't want him to win.

The tone of the evening changed from serious musicality to serious fun when Rylan Clark took to the stage. Performing a mash-up of Eighties artists Duran Duran and Bros, his stage presence was impressive and he had the audience in the palm of his hand. A frustrated Tulisa, however, was disappointed that he hadn't owned the theme of the week as well as she had expected him to. It hadn't lived up to the highs of the previous week. After that, Rylan was expecting the worst from Gary Barlow, the judge who had been the least support-ive of him, and made a wry joke, prompting laughs from the audience. As predicted, Gary had little positive to say, guess-ing that Rylan's burgeoning fame would soon disappear. There was no chance he would win over the Take That star, but did Rylan need his support any more? As the two traded barbs after his performance – with Rylan claiming he didn't play Gary in a Take That tribute band he used to be in as he was 'too skinny' – clearly there was no love lost between them. But it was incredibly entertaining pantomime, and Rylan was becoming more loved by the public every week.

Christopher Maloney embraced the full cheesiness of the evening with a bombastic version of Bonnie Tyler's 'Total Eclipse of the Heart'. Behind him onstage was a huge image of himself, with light pouring eerily out of his eyes – and it freaked Nicole out. Critiquing the bizarre stage prop domi-nated her comments on his performance and she had little good to say about him otherwise. And it was clear that Tulisa, too, was exhausted with relentlessly slamming Christopher. Instead she took the high road with her verdict, praising him for his singing. Rounding off the evening was Jahmene Douglas, adding his soul stylings to The Communards' 'Don't Leave Me This Way'. It was another incredible performance that won all the judges over.

Sunday morning saw Union J wake up more nervous than usual. They had hours to wait until they would find out whether they were staying in the show, but Jaymi's 'coming-out' interview was already published in the *Sun on Sunday*. Over a double-page spread and headlined 'Every boyband needs a gay one, and I'm Union J's', it was a brilliant piece, showcasing Jaymi's upfront and honest nature. 'I came onto the show not wanting to be judged for my personal life,' he told the newspaper. 'But people have caught wind of it and I just wanted to set the record straight. It is not a big thing for me … It is a brave move. There could be negative people, but they are just sad and stuck 20 years ago. I hope the reaction will be, "OK, we kind of knew, but well done on coming out." I don't want people to think I have hidden this to gain votes, because I am so proud of who I am. I hope people respect me for being honest.'

Revealing to the public that his bandmates in Union J had always known, Jaymi explained how important their friendship was to him: 'They have always supported me with doing this. I didn't want to do it in five years' time when I have made money and had a career. I don't think anyone should have to hide who they are.' Jaymi also confessed that the text from the young fan had affected him deeply, reminding him of his younger self. 'I was that kid at 14 and really wish I had someone to say it was OK to be pictured on the red carpet with a guy and be gay in a boyband,' he said. 'I want to have fun with my life. If I can help just one kid out there, that is enough for me.' With such a sensitive and supportive published interview, he was pleased with how it had gone. But would the reaction of his friends and fans be just as understanding?

He needn't have worried for a moment. As Jaymi's news travelled around the Web, the Twittersphere kicked into action and soon he was trending at number one worldwide. Fans flooded the band's feed with messages of love and support. The Union J boys were one of the first with a sweet message for their bandmate: 'Wanted to say how proud we are of our brother Jaymi for coming out and being proud of his sexuality! We are SO proud. Josh, JJ, G' Thousands of tweets on the topic were sent and they were overwhelmingly supportive. 'Well done to Jaymi from @UnionJworld for coming out, nothing at all to be ashamed of and inspiring other people all around the world,' read one, with another saying, 'OMG Jaymi @UnionJWorld well done hun, we love you no matter what.' Even those who weren't huge Union J fans wanted to show that they respected Jaymi for being honest: 'Not too big on @UnionJworld but is actually proud of Jaymi for coming out. Not many people have the balls to do it. Congrats Jaymi.' Even the international media who wouldn't have seen the band on the UK *X Factor* picked up on the story. A piece on Examiner.com held Jaymi up as an example to others. 'Most gay members of boybands come out after their fame has peaked. But Hensley has come out even before Union J has a record deal. It's a brave and commendable step in a world where non-heterosexuals still face a lot of prejudice and are still fighting for equal rights in society,' wrote Carla Hay on the American website. A thrilled and delighted Jaymi wrote a reply on the UnionJWorld Twitter feed: 'Wow, I reeally wasn't expecting this much love! Thank you so much for your supportive messages! Love you all, Jaymi #touched.'

It couldn't have gone better for Jaymi and Union J. Their fans had rallied round and even non-fans were impressed at him standing up for who he was and what he believed in. Whatever happened that night on the results show, they could go in feeling on top of the world. But just a few hours later, it was time to hear whether they would be going through, and once again Union J were on edge. They were back onstage at the Fountain Studios to hear Dermot O'Leary announce the results. He ramped up the tension with an elongated pause before announcing the name of the first safe act. It was them! It was an incredible moment – the boys leaping up and down onstage while Louis congratulated them. They had escaped the bottom two and made it one step closer to the *X Factor* Final.

And the shocks didn't end there. The next name to be called out was Rylan's, and even the lanky star couldn't believe it. He had been expecting to go, but this year's *X Factor* contest certainly wasn't following its expected route. Next up was Jahmene, meaning Christopher was left onstage with Ella and James – two of the judges' clear favourites. Unbelievably, Christopher made it through, so James or Ella would be leaving the competition. Cries of alarm echoed through the studio as a terrified Ella took to the stage for her sing-off number. Trembling with emotion, she performed 'If You're Not the One' by Daniel Bedingfield, followed by James covering Alicia Keys's 'Fallin'.

It was time for the judges to call it. All four of them – as well as Dermot – were still in shock. The host made it clear that he thought it was a huge surprise that two of the most talented contestants were up for the chop. And Tulisa was even more impassioned than usual, as she had to choose between her remaining mentee and the fantastic James Arthur. Declaring that the viewer votes were going the wrong way, she made clear her disgust at what was going to happen that night before saving her own act. Obviously, she had to save Ella and send James home, but her anger was palpable. An emotional Nicole was in complete agreement with her fellow judge. She naturally protected James, her mentee, and sent Ella home, but felt that the result of tonight's phone vote was wildly off course. It was down to Louis and Gary. After championing Ella since the beginning, Louis decided he wanted to send James home. How would Gary vote? Like everyone else, he was going to have to make a painful decision – but Gary plumped for James Arthur as his favourite for the *X Factor* crown. Yet again, it was deadlock with the judges, so the public would decide. Looking devastated, Dermot had the unenviable task of reading out who had garnered the least public phone votes. It was Ella – she was leaving the show. No one could have been happy at the result that week. As the final grew ever closer, the atmosphere on *The X Factor* was becoming increasingly intense. Hugely talented contestants were leaving. How long could Union J survive this cut-throat world?

CHAPTER 11

GETTING CLOSER: THE QUARTER-FINALS, WEEK EIGHT

U nion J, and the rest of the nation, couldn't believe it – Ella Henderson was gone. After being the hot favourite to win the competition, her departure had come as a huge shock to the *X Factor* finalists. They were all competing for a place in the Final, but had expected that, even if they made it, Ella would be there alongside them. As she arrived backstage on the Sunday night following her eviction, the Union J boys were in floods of tears as they went to hug their friend. Seeing her good friends was the moment that finally made Ella cry as she realised she was saying goodbye to the incredible experience that had brought them together. Still, she was looking on the bright side, and to the fact that they would all be reunited on the *X Factor* tour the next year. And Ella promised she would support her best pals all the way to the Final, putting her support behind Union J. Of course, the boys were completely floored by the news, too – that it had been James Arthur and Ella in the bottom two. 'We were just in absolute shock,' Josh told the *Sun*. 'It was bittersweet for us, because we were chuffed to get through, but they are our two best friends in the show. We got so close, so we were devastated – it was like watching your big brother and your little sister in the sing-off.' Jaymi crystallised what Union J had been through – going from being delighted at making it through to being plunged into despair saying goodbye to Ella in just a few moments.

The public reaction to Ella's departure took a nasty turn, with some Twitter users sending death threats to Christopher Maloney. *The X Factor* was used to grabbing headlines each year, but this time around there was a sour feeling about Christopher's involvement in the competition. He himself gave interviews in which he accused *X Factor* bosses of trying to manipulate the public vote against him. 'It seems like underhand tactics are being used to paint a false picture of me and sway the public vote,' he told the *Sunday Mirror*. 'I am the opposite of diva. I mean, I spent most of my life doing shopping for my nan.'

Still, the boys took some time to feel positive about what had happened to them – they were now in the Quarter-Finals of *The X Factor*! They were marvelling at just how far they'd come – even in their wildest dreams they hadn't imagined this would happen to them. But now the boys wanted to go all the way. 'The aim of the game is to win it, and that's it, and that's what we want to do,' Jaymi told the *Sun*. 'I don't think there's anything stopping us from getting to the Final because James and Ella were in the bottom two and we weren't. So to be above them – and yes, people might have thought they were safe – we're doing something right. We want to fight for this. And based upon how much we want it and how hard we work, I don't see why we can't get to the Final.'

That past weekend, Jaymi also had to deal with the aftermath of his coming-out interview – and was overwhelmed by the positive reaction. 'It's been amazing, really amazing. I have not seen one negative comment,' he told the *Sun*. 'I want to say a massive thank you for people's support. It has been incredible. I have already had messages from young gay guys saying "thank you so much, I can look up to you", and that's what I did it for.' Originally he had wanted to keep his partner Olly out of the media spotlight, but it proved impossible as fans tracked him down. Jaymi conceded it had turned out for the best. 'Olly has got loads of messages,' he continued. 'I always knew people would find him, but he is totally overwhelmed with the support. It's really uplifting.' He further explained to *The X Factor* that week why he'd not spoken about it before then – he had wanted to be judged on his own merits, not on his private life. It wasn't everything about him.

On this high note, the boys were ready for some festive fun. With Christmas just around the corner, they were in the mood for the launch of Winter Wonderland, an annual outdoor attraction in London's Hyde Park, featuring a Christmas market, ice rink, big-top shows and fairground rides. Flashbulbs popped as Union J and the rest of the *X Factor* family joined celebrities such as Katie Price to soak up the festive atmosphere and enjoy an evening out. 'We're loving it,' Josh told the waiting cameras as the boys grinned, Jaymi togged up for the chilly winter night in a cute fluffy brown bear hat.

Now the relationship between Union J and their fans became closer than ever. The boys regularly posted video diaries on YouTube and always stopped to sign autographs and have their photos taken with the devoted JCats, who waited for them outside the studios despite the bitter winter cold. And their regular Twitcam sessions were taking on cult status. In the latest one, filmed that week, JJ and George dressed in monkey onesies, specially made for them, and invited their fans to give them dares to do – 'We can do whatever you want us to – obviously nothing too rude!' explained JJ. They also gave a great interview to *Heat* magazine, which proclaimed to its readers: 'Get ready to fancy Union J' – if they didn't already do so. Backstage on *The X Factor*, it was time to answer fans' questions and reveal who would be in which 'house' in the *Harry Potter* series. Daydreamer JJ was declared a Hufflepuff boy, George was Gryffindor, while Josh was unanimously placed in Slytherin! He wasn't best pleased with that – and neither was Jaymi to be put in Ravenclaw. Wittily, he declared he wasn't going to be in that house, as the pupils there were never featured on screen.

As the Quarter-Finals drew ever closer, there would be no let-up for Union J on the publicity trail – every viewer's vote counted. The boys made an early-morning appearance on ITV's *Daybreak* with Lorraine Kelly to talk about their experience so far. 'We weren't even supposed to be on Judges' Houses, so to be this far is just mind-blowing,' said Jaymi. They even joked about how their physical rough-and-tumble onstage after making it through each week was taking its toll on Louis Walsh. 'We think it takes him a week to recover, with his bad back!' said Josh. Host Lorraine was clearly a huge fan of the band, and also congratulated Jaymi on his coming out the previous weekend – highlighting the fact that the public hadn't seen it as a big deal. 'That's what I wanted to prove,' explained Jaymi. 'That everyone I've ever met hasn't had an issue with it.' He even revealed that the young fan whose tweet had inspired Jaymi to come out had now done so to his own family. 'So that was a massive thing for me,' he said. 'We're so proud of him,' chipped in JJ, while Josh added: 'He shouldn't hide who he is – because he's Jaymi, he's wicked and we love him.'

At this stage in the competition, each act had even more to do, with two songs to learn for the Saturday night. It was ABBA and Motown Week so they'd be tackling classic tunes beloved by the viewers at home. It was a daunting prospect when, up until now, it had been difficult enough to nail one song perfectly. With it being the Quarter-Finals, they couldn't afford to deliver a below-par performance – the nation would be watching. George joked that they were going to listen to judge Nicole Scherzinger after her criticisms the previous weekend, too – banning plinths from their performance. Wearing a cute bear hat, he promised the cameras that the band had swept boxes out of the picture, and therefore would hopefully win over the former Pussycat Doll. Incredibly, the final was now just two weeks away. And the boys now had a huge test to undertake – double the workload of the previous weeks, which had hardly been a walk in the park.

As the weeks of non-stop hard work caught up with them, the boys looked tired. But, despite this, they were more focused than ever, encouraged to fight ever harder by their mentor Louis. He was incredibly impressed by how the boys had stepped up to the challenges laid in front of them and shown that they were unafraid of hard graft. He had every faith in them that they could make it through.

Saturday night saw a group of very nervous boys take to the stage – with Ella's exit, it was an all-male Quarter-Final. All the competing acts pulled together to perform the group song – Coldplay's 'Viva La Vida'. Despite the rivalry, the acts wanted the best for each other and knew they were facing a huge challenge in the night ahead. A supremely charismatic Rylan Clark took to the stage first, for a housed-up version of ABBA's 'Mamma Mia'. He looked as if he was born to the life of a performer, would his pizzazz and star quality be enough to see him through another week of the contest? 'Louis was ready to deliver a gushing verdict, as he had a whale of a time watching the popular performer. His verdict was 100 per cent positive. Even Gary had decided it was time to call a truce with Rylan. He had been his long-term adversary on the judges' panel, but now, at this late stage, Gary knew Rylan had proved his worth as an *X Factor* contestant and recognised that the viewers at home had show their support for him. A ceasefire between the two was declared, and Rylan even went on to congratulate Gary on his recent OBE. After Rylan's months in the competition, it seemed Gary had finally conceded that there was something about the Essex boy that people adored.

Only a few minutes later, Union J were standing in the spotlight, in front of a backdrop sparkling with atmospheric lights. Jaymi began singing the first familiar 'Whoas' of ABBA's classic tearjerker 'The Winner Takes It All'. In a recent poll, it had been voted the nation's favourite ABBA song of all time, so the pressure was on. Would the boys be able to do it justice? Keeping the staging simple – with no boxes! – and strolling towards the crowd, this was Union J's chance to showcase their vocals and let everyone see how much they'd improved over the course of the competition. Josh and Jaymi shone again, with their powerful, emotive voices taking centre stage. As they finished the number and waited to hear the judges' reactions, they must have hoped that the lyrics and the sentiment of the song would prove their lucky charm.

Tulisa had often been their harshest critic, but tonight she was clearly impressed, highlighting their vocals, staging and performance as all being top quality. Union J smiled at each other – this was starting out well. And it continued in a similar vein, with Gary sensing something big was about to happen. Yet again, his gut feeling was great and he knew that Union J were shaping up to be something special. Jaymi and George grinned and hugged Josh – who looked thrilled – even closer. Gary wished them his best at this crucial point in the competition. With that seal of approval, Union J couldn't help but burst with pride as the screams grew louder in the studio. Nicole noticed it and pointed out that this was something the boys would become increasingly familiar with. Their future was going to include lots of screaming girls, lots of performing and lots of success. It was a fantastic appraisal.

All the judges had sensed a change in Union J over the past few weeks: they had gelled more as a band and now their confidence was palpable. And there were more words of praise to come from Nicole – she bigged up Jaymi for having the strength to publicly come out, and also complimented his musical skills. Louis stepped in to ensure none of his band were missed out. Every single member of the band contributed to their success equally in his view, and yes – it was votes that counted. Allying Union J with fellow *X Factor* boybands One Direction and JLS, Louis knew that the further they went, the more the British public would get behind them in the future. What a reception. It felt as if all four judges were anointing Union J's future and assuring them that a huge pop career lay ahead.

When presenter Dermot O'Leary asked for their reaction, George was so overwhelmed that all he could do was giggle in delight! Josh stepped in, declaring that they were all totally chuffed with the reception. Grinning non-stop, George managed to pull himself together and say a few words of his joy and amazement. Dermot hugged the lads as they moved offstage – all on a high after such a full and positive reaction. But unlike previous weeks, this time they wouldn't be able to kick back and relax backstage, watching the other acts: in a short while, they had another number to perform.

Meanwhile, Jahmene Douglas performed 'I Have a Dream', which seemed to resonate personally with the singer due to his tough upbringing. Although the song wasn't something that Jahmene would normally have wanted to sing, which Louis noted, he managed to turn it into a superb soul number. Louis declared that Jahmene should make it through to next week's Final – something that Tulisa and Nicole both agreed with, concurring that Jahmene did have the most impressive voice of all. Union J knew Jahmene would be hard to beat. Humble, sweet and possessed of an enormous talent, he had a huge following.

After his shocking appearance in the bottom two the previous week, James Arthur was no longer assured of a smooth path to the Final. He knew he had to impress even more than usual, and delivered a raw, emotional version of ABBA's 'SOS', transforming it from a disco track into a mid-tempo rock number. It was a surprising combination, but once again the creative singer showed he was able to pull off the most unusual mash-ups. Tulisa, who now had none of her own acts left in the show, congratulated him on another awesome performance – and publicly stated that she now wanted either him or Jahmene to win. Union J woudn't be getting her vote when it came to the crunch.

So far the judges had been fulsome in their praise of every act who'd performed – the standard was now so high, it was getting harder to criticise. But last up was Christopher Maloney. Surrounded by near-naked dancers, he sang ABBA's atmospheric 'Fernando', using his powerful voice to full extent. Looking pained, Nicole offered up some faint compliments before delivering her final verdict – although it had impressed her visually, with the dancers and the spectacle, she'd found the actual number really boring. Louis made another dig at Christopher, thanking him for not stripping down to his underwear! This riled a frustrated Gary, who urged Louis to stick to criticising the music, not his personality. With Tulisa declaring the performance unsettling in the extreme, it was clear that Christopher was still far from any support on the judges' panel.

Now it was time for the finalists to take on some much-loved Motown numbers. Perhaps predictably, Rylan went for a mash-up of The Supremes' greatest hits, which saw him strut throughout the studio audience and end with a dare-devil leap into a dancer's arms. But once again, Rylan's magic had failed to work on the judges, with Louis proclaiming it a miss – although the deafening chants from the crowd seemed to suggest otherwise. All the judges – apart from Rylan's mentor Nicole, who gave him another crazy nick-name – appeared underwhelmed by his second performance. He was clearly at risk.

Union J were about to take to the stage to cover the Jackson 5's 'I'll Be There'. They knew that performing a song by a young Michael Jackson and his brothers was a big ask – the group had been one of the biggest boybands ever in the 1970s and their songs still lived on. Of course, Michael Jackson had gone on to become a legendary global superstar, so Union J knew they would have to knock it out of the park. As the bandmate with arguably the best voice, Jaymi took the lead vocals, soon joined by Josh and the rest of the boys. It was an affecting, epic performance, with the crowd behind the boys all the way, waving their arms in time. Were they set for as fabulous a reception as last time from the judges?

With Tulisa's first words, they could be in no doubt. She was clearly impressed beyond measure that they had pulled it off – and stated in her direct way that they had never had a better night in *The X Factor* so far. But Gary would prove harder to please. In his opinion, they had squandered an opportunity to do something spectacular. Explaining that, as boybands had originated from Motown, and with Union J being a boyband themselves, he thought the synergy between the two eras could have been much more original. Again, he laid the blame at Louis's door for failing to encourage the band to think outside the box. His criticisms were directed at their mentor rather than the boys themselves, as Gary clearly thought highly of Union J, but his words didn't go down well. Nicole disagreed straight away, pointing out that the hordes of fans screaming for Union J would want to listen to their version again and again. Talking to a beaming Union J, she complimented their simple, pure singing and delivery. It was up to Louis to deliver the remaining boost the boys needed – hailing it as their most impressive singing and accusing Gary of lacking clear hearing! He finished by urging the votes to go Union J's way. Yet again, Louis displayed his concern that, despite all the praise and cheers, the boys could still find themselves in the bottom two.

Dermot O'Leary was now up onstage and ready to call in Gary's comments after he'd criticised Louis earlier for not focusing on Christopher's vocals. Gary stuck by his point – Union J should have been more innovative in their interpretation of the number. Jaymi stepped up to the plate to explain their position. The Luton singer insisted articulately that the band had found their niche and, after many weeks of exploring their options, believed they'd finally found a sound that defined them as a band.

Jahmene Douglas proved he was much more at home with Motown with his second song, 'The Tracks of My Tears' by Smokey Robinson & The Miracles. Again the judges couldn't find any reason to criticise Jahmene, with Louis declaring that he would be a Motown star if the label were still going. Meanwhile, James Arthur gave free rein to his sexy side, with Marvin Gaye's classic 'Let's Get It On', singing directly to

Nicole and his cheering fans in the crowd. It displayed an angle to the singer that hadn't been seen before, and he totally blitzed it. For Louis, there had been no better show-case that evening, and Nicole cheekily inferred that couples might start to feel romantic after watching James's perfor-mance! Rounding off the evening was Christopher Maloney, singing Lionel Richie's 'Dancing on the Ceiling'. Looking resigned, he took the judges' criticisms on the chin, as he was yet again dismissed as a karaoke singer by the panel.

Just 24 hours later, all the judges – minus Tulisa, with no acts left in the show – took to the stage with their protégés to learn who had made it through to the Semi-Finals. James Arthur was announced first, and after his exceptional perfor-mance, it felt like a shoo-in. Also through was Christopher Maloney, leaving Louis utterly surprised as he pulled a 'What?' face, waiting next to Union J. With the Scouse singer through, it now meant that one of the judges' preferred acts would be in the bottom two. With so few acts left, there was only one more safe space. Jaymi bowed his head, consumed with nerves. The final safe spot would go to … Jahmene Douglas.

They were in the bottom two: the dreaded situation had reared its ugly head again. Union J huddled into a tight group as they rallied together. Up against Rylan Clark, however, they had a real chance to deliver a storming performance that would see them through. Rylan was first up, performing an emotional version of 'Wires' by Athlete. The camp crazi-ness was gone and instead he showcased his honest, heartfelt side. When he'd previously done so, with 'Kissing You' in Week Five, he had been saved. Would the magic work again?

Union J whistled and cheered on their friend. The evening now filled with melancholy — even if the boys made it through, their friend would be leaving the show.

For the third time, the boys drew on all their resources to make it through the sing-off. Their song was 'Run', the epic ballad by Snow Patrol. They delivered a passionate, earnest performance, knowing this could be their last moment on the *X Factor* stage. Without a doubt, they had the edge on Rylan, but would the judges agree? Time to find out. While the Union J boys gazed at the floor in adrenalin-fuelled terror, Rylan stood, head-up, awaiting the news with a small smile. It was bound to be bad news for the boys first off as Nicole gave her verdict — she had enjoyed their sincere performance, but as her act was Rylan, her loyalty lay with him. She was sending them home. Graciously, the four lads clapped as Dermot moved on to their own mentor, Louis. Again, the result was predictable; despite his praise for Rylan, whose personality had bound the *X Factor* family together, Louis was not going to abandon his boys. In his opinion, too, they'd won the sing-off with sheer talent.

With the predicted votes out of the way, the tension ramped up as Gary and Tulisa were about to call it. Would the sing-off go to deadlock? Would they favour Rylan? Or would Union J be safe? Gary, who'd long been very much in the anti-Rylan camp, began his speech by praising Union J for delivering terrific performances over the weekend. He predicted that, before long, record labels would be clamouring to sign the band. When it came to Rylan, he also delivered some kind words about his performance and clarified that none of their onstage banter had had a nasty angle to it.

But his opinion hadn't changed – he was going to send Rylan home.

With Gary's support, Union J knew the judges wouldn't be sending them home – either they'd now go through or Tulisa would take the vote to deadlock. Which would it be? It would be hard to call, as she had often been a critic of the four boys. She began by weighing up the two acts' various plus points, but was chivvied along by Dermot to make a decision as the show drew to a close. It was time for Tulisa to call it – and for Union J to face the biggest moment of their career so far. It was the most nervous and frightened they had ever felt. Full of apologies, Tulisa decided on the act that she thought had the most potential in the future – Union J. Rylan was out!

Close to tears, George buried his face in Josh's shoulder as the boys moved over to embrace Rylan. It was a moment charged with joy and sadness. And Union J walked one step closer to the Final.

CHAPTER 12

HEARTBREAK: THE SEMI-FINALS

'Thank you so much for voting for us! As you can tell, we're totally shocked. Please keep voting and keep us here, we love it so much.' It was late Sunday night, after the results of Week Eight's live show, and an emotional Jaymi decided to record a message for the fans and post it on UnionJWorld's Twitter feed. JJ and Josh also took time to record quick messages of thanks for their fans, against the noisy backdrop of the aftershow party. 'A massive thank you to all the JCats out there for keeping our dream alive! Please, please, still pick up the phone and vote – we're so close to the Final,' JJ urged. Josh's video message was: 'Hello to you amazing JCats out there, I just want to say a huge, huge thank you to everyone who's voted, to everyone who's supported us. We love you so much – without you, nothing would be possible – and fingers crossed we'll be in the Final!' In fact, all the members of Union J were knocked for six. They couldn't believe they'd made it to the Semi-Finals of *The X Factor*, but yet again it had been agony getting there, once more ending up in the bottom two and knowing they weren't one of the most popular remaining acts.

Rylan Clark had left amid a flurry of offers to appear on other shows – *Celebrity Big Brother*, *Benidorm*, *TOWIE* and even a presenting stint on *Daybreak* were laid at the lanky singer's door. *The X Factor* was opening new doors for the Essex celebrity, who discovered that his genuine charm and sense of fun had found favour with the British public. But without his bubbly personality around to inject a big dose of craziness, Union J really missed him. With so few people left in the competition, George found that things felt a little bit flatter than before. Now the focus was entirely on the Final and who was going make it. The atmosphere had changed. The competition had become 100 per cent about one thing only.

Things were definitely getting serious. But as one of the final five, Union J had to prepare for the reality that they might actually win the competition. It seemed such an amazing possibility after all they'd been through over the past few months. They wanted to make it as much as ever, but having been in the bottom two more than any of the other acts there – Jahmene, for example, had never found himself in that position – they knew how vulnerable they were. To the boys, the week felt busier than ever, but yet again they had to prepare two incredible songs to perform in the Semi-Final. Jaymi fretted about whether their voices, having gone through such strain over the past few weeks, were up to it, but they managed to work well together. He also felt that they'd learned an awful lot about their lives from going on the *X Factor* journey – the boys now felt destined to remain together as a group and knew that, with application and hard work, they could achieve pretty much anything!

Worryingly, there was now the distinct chance that Christopher Maloney could end up the victor. Despite being at the bottom of the judges' list, he kept returning week after week – leading show boss Simon Cowell to take matters into his own hands. He urged his five million Twitter followers to vote for a credible act, without ever naming who he thought was deserving of a place in the Final and who wasn't. And Simon's close friend Sinitta again spoke to the press about his concerns. 'The wrong people are going. He finds it frustrating,' she told the *People*. Having Christopher remain in the competition was seen as damaging to the credibility of *The X Factor* – something that was reported in the *Sun* as the show's producers began to make plans for the Final. 'In the past, *The X Factor* has attracted big names to duet with its wannabes during the Final, including Beyoncé, Rihanna, Kylie Minogue and Robbie Williams,' said the newspaper. 'But producers have struggled to find anyone willing to sing with Christopher as he is seen as too uncool – unlike the other acts still in the competition, such as James Arthur, Jahmene Douglas and boyband Union J.' In the end, the producers decided to team up all the finalists with judges instead of celebrity guests. Whether Christopher was the reason for this remained unclear.

With the Final just around the corner, interest in Union J was at fever pitch that week. If the boys thought it had been crazy so far, now they were truly public property. With conversations revolving around who wanted who to win *The X Factor* (or even rival show *Strictly Come Dancing*), Union J's name was on everyone's lips. Naturally, everybody wanted to know about the lads' love lives – and with Jaymi the only one who was attached, there was plenty on which to speculate. After spending weeks denying the Ella Henderson rumours, headlines hit the Web that George was in fact in a text relationship with someone he knew back home. In an interview with *Heat* magazine, the truth came out – thanks to bandmate Jaymi! Asked whether he was texting someone he liked, George simply replied, 'Nope.' 'Yes you are!' insisted Jaymi, with George eventually admitting, 'I am actually texting someone. No one you'd know.' Just a day later, snaps appeared in the tabloids of George leaving his now-regular party haunt Mahiki, holding hands with a 'mystery blonde'. No details emerged as to who the lucky girl was, but since Ella told *Look* magazine, 'After the competition, I'd love to see him … you can't help how you feel about someone,' she must surely have been feeling a bit disappointed.

But it wasn't just George whose private life was hitting the headlines. Quietest Union J lad JJ was suddenly splashed all over the newspapers after supposedly going on dates with one of the *X Factor*'s backing dancers. Brazilian Rithy Periera, who had also appeared on Fox's *So You Think You Can Dance*, was said to have met JJ backstage on the show and gone out with him for dinner. 'Now he's really into her,' claimed the *Sun*. But JJ denied it all straight away on *The Xtra Factor*, insisting that he was single and the pair were just friends, nothing more. Although his words might have given hope to reams of Union J fans, there was no chance the boys would be able to deny some of the other photos that cropped up in the press that week. JJ and Josh were photographed outside their hotel in the early hours of Thursday morning after a night on the town with James Arthur accompanied by some gorgeous blonde girls. Despite the pressure on them for the coming weekend, the boys were determined to have some fun – and they deserved it.

It had been over a week since Jaymi had come out about his sexuality – and the positive reactions continued to pour in. He was incredibly moved by the stories he was hearing, and the realisation that he could have such a huge impact on fans' lives humbled him. 'I've been getting an absolutely amazing reaction from both teenage girls and young gay guys that are struggling with their sexuality,' he told Sugarscape. com. 'The main reason I did it was I was at a stage when I was younger that I didn't have anyone to look up to. I always wished there was someone honest and open about it, and I thought, "Who am I to sit here and not give that to these kids?"' He'd been especially affected by one story, where a Union J fan's brother had been really depressed and down. Since Jaymi came out, however, he'd found the courage to tell his sister about his sexuality and they had bonded over it. For Jaymi, this was a life-changing experience as he realised he was becoming a much-loved role model, helping young people come to terms with their sexuality.

As the Semi-Final took place on 1 December 2012 and the nation had just opened the first window on their Advent calendar, the X Factor producers decided to give the Saturday-night show a festive theme. For the group song that week they even boasted a celebrity guest, rocker Rod Stewart, to sing 'Merry Christmas, Baby' with the remaining contestants. The boys looked especially gorgeous that night, dressed in simple, stylish black suits. However, beneath the surface, as JJ said later, they'd had a funny feeling all day that things wouldn't go perfectly. But they weren't about to let this affect their performance, with Jaymi again delivering standout vocals alongside the legendary Stewart. It was a fun, festive start to the show, but afterwards things immediately got serious.

Showing off his strong voice, Christopher Maloney performed Josh Groban's 'You Raise Me Up' as his first song choice. With his bombastic, operatic delivery, it was perfect for the Scouse singer – but what would the judges say? Nicole was the first to speak and, amazingly, she was full of gushing praise for his voice. What was this – compliments from the judges? Christopher, and the viewers at home, were stunned. And it didn't end there. Louis was straight in with the fulsome praise as well – giving him credit for singing a song his timbre was ideally suited to and for having got so far in a tough competition. Louis even predicted that Christopher might have a future on the stage. Even Tulisa was pleased, telling him how fun she'd found it. It was a staggering about-face for the judges, who up until then seemed to have done their utmost to profess how sick of his 'cheesy' style they were. Some reports in the press claimed that their constant criticism was turning Christopher into an underdog figure, with people voting for him because they felt sorry for him. Was this an attempt to reverse all that? Either way, the singer left the stage much happier than he'd ever done before.

With Jahmene Douglas's performance of 'I Look to You' by Whitney Houston getting across-the-board rave reviews – even bringing Nicole to tears – the minutes before Union J's first appearance flew by. With the theme for the first song being Songs for Someone Special, they'd chosen 'Beneath

Your Beautiful' by Emeli Sandé and Labrinth. With dramatic shards of light shining on each boy, it felt like the moment they became the stars they'd always been destined to become. Josh took lead vocals for the opening verse, the emotion painted all over his face. With George's guitar playing, Jaymi's passionate vocal stylings and JJ's steady presence, it was a magical moment for Union J. And the moment hit home with the judges, too – Tulisa recognised that it meant a transition point for the band. They had grown so much in the competition and were now ready for even more challenges. She was effusive in her compliments yet again.

They'd even managed to win over Gary Barlow, whose bugbear about their voices working together was finally about to be laid to rest. Not only did he congratulate them on their song and vocal stylings, he also thought they'd finally nailed the 'blending' issue that had dogged them in the past. Now they truly sounded like a united band and their onstage confidence was clear. Like the other judges had said before, Gary believed that big things would be coming Union J's way after this, whether they won or not. George shrugged his shoulders and grinned disbelievingly; the others looked as if they felt secure in their future. Whatever the result from that night, everyone could see that Union J had an exciting future ahead. Nicole was on side, too. She credited the four boys for being able to deliver a soaring ballad without descending into mawkishness, and highlighted Josh's voice getting better and better, too. Over screams from the audience, Louis also wanted to point out how international Union J's appeal was becoming. Not only were the boys taking over the UK, they had also appeared on *The Late Late*

Show in Dublin, Ireland, to the same hysterical screams from fans. It felt like his forecast was finally turning true – Union J were indeed shaping up to become huge stars.

Dermot O'Leary affectionately took the mickey out of Louis as he leapt onto the stage to speak to the boys. With George again giggling too much to speak, it was down to Josh to pick up the mic. The boys were thrilled with the opinions of all the judges, whom they all held in really high esteem. Again, Josh flagged up how much effort they'd put in. Almost overcome with the occasion, the band left the stage to take stock of the terrific reception they'd received – and to get themselves ready for their next performance. Only James Arthur was left to perform and he put his own spin on a pop classic, something he was fast becoming known for. He took on U2's 'One' and turned it into a soulful, trip-hop number. It was enough for Tulisa to lavish her most extravagant praise yet on him. She proclaimed that it was time for an artist like James Arthur to finally win a huge national competiton like *The X Factor*. She ended her rapture with a call to arms: the public should vote for James Arthur to win.

With Tulisa pinning her colours to the mast for James, Nicole supporting her boys, James and Jahmene, and Gary behind his act, Christopher, Union J had only Louis as the judge who clearly wanted them to win. But as the judges didn't have any influence that week, with the results decided entirely by phone votes, the boys focused on making it all about their performance. It was time for each act to deliver their second track, and Christopher Maloney attempted a cover of Michael Bublé's 'Haven't Met You Yet'. After the rapturous reception afforded him for his first song, this one would not receive the same reaction. It had been disappointing, sighed Nicole. She saved her real ire for Gary, blaming him for giving Christopher such a hard song to tackle. Although Gary defended his act, the buzz around Christopher from earlier on had quickly faded. There were no such worries with Jahmene when he came out with the song he'd sung at his first audition for *The X Factor* – Etta James's 'At Last'. Gary was ready to declare it the song that should take Jahmene all the way to the Final next week – it had been truly amazing.

It was Union J's last performance of the night. They'd chosen Lonestar's 'I'm Already There', a country music track about loved ones being kept apart by long distance. In a big change to their usual style, George took on solo vocals for the first few lines, and then handed over to Josh. The boys performed the song with every inch of their being as it built to a powerful crescendo and ended on a beautiful harmony. They hugged each other tightly – that was it. They couldn't do any more to try to secure a place in the Final. But, sadly, Tulisa's reception was muted. She had been impressed with their singing, but again accused them of not mixing things up enough. For the opinionated judge, there had been too little difference between the two performances, although she conceded that Union J really had put in more hard work than anyone at home could see. She hadn't said anything particularly bad, but this was far from the rave reviews she'd been giving James and Jahmene. Would Gary think any differently?

It wasn't to be. He was also disappointed with what they'd done – it was too predictable, not exciting enough. Just like last week, when he'd called them out for not making enough of the Motown boyband opportunity, Gary was again warning the boys that they might have blown their chances. In his opinon, they were at risk of ending up in the bottom two again. Union J looked devastated. Their shoulders slumped as they digested what Gary had said. With the exceptional talent demonstrated by James and Jahmene, and the level of public support given to Christopher, they knew they had an uphill struggle ahead.

Still, there was Nicole left to speak, and she boosted their spirits straight away, declaring that she had adored it. Full of her quirky words, her speech bigged up Louis as the boys' mentor for finding what it was they had and encouraging the boys to work hard. She had really enjoyed their performance and reminded them of what was most important – they had made it to the Semi-Finals of *The X Factor*! Nicole had put the smile back on Union J's faces. Louis then stepped in with his repetitious call to the viewers to help support the band by voting for them. After a dig at Tulisa for not having any acts left, Louis even promised he would wear a onesie if it meant Union J would stay in.

So what did Jaymi make of the accusation that the song was a safe choice? He accepted that, for some of the judges, that was so, but the track had been an important one for the band. The sentiment of the song had been about missing loved ones, which was something they could clearly identify with after so many weeks of being away from home. Appearing stricken with nerves and uncertainty, Union J left the stage to watch James Arthur's last effort. He sang 'The Power of Love' by Frankie Goes to Hollywood with real hurt and heartbreak, leading the judges to get to their feet in a standing ovation. If the viewers at home thought no more praise could be heaped on the singer, they were wrong, as Gary declared there had been no better performance yet.

The Saturday-night showdown had ended on a huge high, but now Sunday loomed as D-Day for all the remaining contestants. Just three acts would make it through to the coveted Final, to be held in Manchester on the following Saturday night. Looking more relaxed than their rivals as they strode onstage, Union J waited to hear. There would be no judges' votes and no sing-off: this was it.

Josh shut his eyes as he waited to hear Dermot speak. The first act through was James. The singer punched the air and whooped in delight. So who would be joining him in the Final? George looked terrified, and Josh put a comforting arm around him. The name was called out – Christopher! It was the shock that everyone had expected – after getting him through this far, Christopher's public support had seen him all the way to the Final. Now it was down to Jahmene and Union J. Jaymi bowed his head and JJ kept his hands in his pockets. This was it. The last place in the *X Factor* Final would be taken by … Jahmene.

With those words, Union J's *X Factor* dream was over. After months of devoting everything they had – and then some – to the competition, they hadn't managed to conquer the last hurdle. All the finalists ran to give each other supportive hugs, as Dermot pulled the Union J boys back for their exit interview. He knew the band had been feeling unsettled all day, convinced that their *X Factor* journey would end tonight. And so it had proved, but how did everything feel now it had happened? As Josh's voice cracked with emotion, he simply explained how amazing it felt to have got so far and how grateful they were to the show for giving them this opportunity. And, ever the gentlemen, Union J offered the remaining finalists their best wishes. Louis was right behind his boys. Covering his disappointment well, he again proclaimed them the stars of the future with a big shout. The other judges laughed – Louis had been saying the same thing for weeks. Jaymi closed Union J's exit with a few more heartfelt words – this had been the culmination of so many years of hopes raised and dashed, and it had been better than any of them could have expected.

The VT rolled, showing Union J's 'best bits': from their nervous audition moments to the early days of the group as a four-piece and their incredible time on *The X Factor*, with their fanbase and confidence growing week on week. The boys took to the stage for the last time, singing Taylor Swift's 'Love Story' to a rapturous crowd. It was clear that, although this might be the end of one journey, it was also the beginning of another.

CHAPTER 13

AFTERMATH: LIFE AFTER THE LIVE SHOWS

'We're gutted we're not in the Final.' In the days following their *X Factor* eviction, this was a sentiment Union J found themselves repeating over and over again. They might have left the competition, but the next few days found them more in demand than ever, doing countless rounds of interviews on TV and online. Of course, they took to Twitter straight away to shout out to their fans after Sunday night's eviction, writing: 'Best experience of my life! Thank you so much to everyone who has supported us. So far!! See you soon! George. X' An emotional Josh later added: 'Wanted to say thank you to everyone who got us 4th! We hope you all continue to support us. Fingers crossed this isn't the last of us. Josh. x' Thousands of retweets and comments showed that the JCats were still 100 per cent behind them. '@unionjworld well done for getting so far <3 you did us all sooo proud & you're gonna have a great career ahead! #weloveyouunionj <3' wrote one fan, with thousands echoing her sentiments. They'd left on a tide of goodwill. Everyone was behind them, willing them to go on and build an amazing career.

So Monday morning didn't see a lie-in for Union J, despite Sunday night's results. An early wake-up call was in order for the boys to head to the London Studios on the Southbank to appear on *Daybreak* – the first of many interviews that day. And one familiar face was there to make the boys feel at home: Rylan! Covering the holiday of usual entertainment presenter Richard Arnold, he impressed his friends with his confident presenting style. 'Unfortunately someone had to leave, and it was my four little brothers, Union J,' he told presenter Lorraine Kelly before the boys came on. Looking sleep-deprived but relaxed, Union J settled into talking about their *X Factor* journey coming to an end. 'We've had the best time of our lives,' said Josh. Lorraine and her fellow presenter Aled Jones wanted to know what was next for the boys. 'I think we'll firstly take a few days to go and see our families and get some sleep!' laughed Jaymi. 'But this is not the end of us at all. We want to try and pursue a deal, write an album – that's what the dream is and this has been an amazing stepping stone.' 'I've got to say, these are four of the nicest and politest boys ever. They've got such a good future,' chipped in Rylan with some encouraging – and warning – words. 'And I know you say you're going to have a couple of days off to sleep … Babe, you're not! It's going to be a lot of work.' He was joking, but there was a serious point to be made: the boys might be coming off the *X Factor* treadmill, but they were stepping onto another.

There was only time to grab a quick breakfast before moving into the *This Morning* studios for another TV appearance. The interview marked the closing of a circle for Union J: the first time they'd appeared on the show, over two months before, presenter Eamonn Holmes had needed cue cards to tell him who was who. Now presenters Holly Willoughby and Phillip Schofield knew exactly who each member of Union J was, just like most of the country. Sitting with the *Xtra Factor* host Caroline Flack, the boys tried to make the best of their departure, and explained why they had felt their time was up. 'We've also been in the bottom two a fair few times, which doesn't fill you with confidence,' Josh wryly observed. 'And of course the judges aren't there to save you; James and Jahmene are amazing and Christopher's getting all the votes. He's fantastic as well.' But like everyone else, Phillip knew that the band would go on to huge success anyway. 'Absolutely,' agreed Caroline. 'You've got to see the size of their fanbase outside the studios. And you've only got to look at someone like Cher Lloyd, who's doing amazingly in the States, who came fourth. One Direction came third.'

Union J were definitely following an esteemed group of successful acts who hadn't won *The X Factor*, but there was still one reason why the boys were disappointed they hadn't made the Final: Louis had promised to wear a onesie if they'd been successful! 'There was talk of him even wearing a leotard in the Final,' said Jaymi, with JJ adding, 'Yeah, we were talking about doing the Riverdance with him, too!' The boys might have had Louis's unwavering cheerleading, but Holly wanted to know what Gary's words meant to them. 'He's been a massive support to us, because he's an amazing judge and songwriter. Every week he gave us maybe a little bit of criticism, but that's what made us better. We wanted to stand up against James and Jahmene and didn't want to be seen as a weak act, so it's down to the judges' comments that have made us go away and work at what we needed to work on,' explained Jaymi.

Of course, with the fans and the press in uproar about their departure while Christopher Maloney headed towards the Final, the boys were relentlessly grilled about their opinions on the former cruise-ship singer. 'It's weird, because James and Jahmene are incredible, and Chris is incredible with what he does, but I felt that maybe there were more people that were more relevant and current,' hedged Jaymi, when questioned by *ITN News*. 'This year's been such a current year, artistry-wise, it wouldn't be the step forward the show really needed to get away from the past few years, where people said it was karaoke, the same every year. This year's been so different, I think it would be a shame if someone like James or Jahmene didn't win – to give the show a new life for the future and future series.' 'But, of course, we say fair play to him,' added JJ. 'Oh, definitely,' agreed Jaymi. And who did Union J think would end up with the winner's spoils on Saturday night? 'Chris!' declared Josh, Jaymi and JJ, although George piped up with 'Jahmene.' 'Chris will win, although we want James or Jahmene to win,' said Josh. 'I've just had a feeling all series about this,' explained Jaymi. 'I think as soon as he got a wild card, I said to someone he was going to win.' Would Mystic Jaymi's prediction come true? They had only a few days to wait to find out.

Talking about the previous night's experience all day helped Union J process what had happened to them. And the more they talked about it, the more they realised that it didn't matter so much that they hadn't made it to the Final. After all, as they said to their interviewers, they'd been expecting it. 'We kind of had that gut feeling all day. We weren't shocked. We were gutted, but we weren't shocked,' JJ told *ITN News*.

For Jaymi, hearing that they were out of *The X Factor* had even given him a huge sense of relief. 'For me personally, when they said Jahmene, it felt like a lot of pressure was lifted off my shoulders,' he explained. 'It felt like that *X Factor* bubble had popped and we were now ready to go out and prove ourselves. The last 10 weeks haven't even been half the battle – the rest of the battle is to go out and get a record deal, write some songs, get the songs out, hit Number One, sell a tour out. All these other things you need to get stressed about, this has set us up so well for that. It's literally been the best experience of our lives.' And speaking to the *Sun* newspaper later on, Jaymi confirmed his opinion that it had actually served Union J better to go out when they did. 'Nine times out of ten it is actually better not to win. It is exciting times for Union J,' he told the newspaper. 'We get the option to really work on our artistry. We get the time but not the pressure of being the winners to really sit down and work out what style of music we want to do and make us a brand. We have got a lot of positives out of this and they outweigh the negatives.'

There was another big change in store for the group that week. After spending every spare moment they had at the glamorous Corinthia hotel – home to all the *X Factor* finalists that year – it was time to move out. 'It's going to be weird not living with each other,' said Jaymi on *This Morning*. 'We've been living together day and night for the last three months, so going home to our own bedrooms is going to be really weird.' For Union J, it marked the end of an era – the hotel had been where they'd bonded and grown as a band. Now they were moving into a new life as a group and, although there would be countless more hotels in their future, they'd never have this intense experience again. Josh clearly found it a special moment when they finally packed up their suitcases and walked out of those super-swanky doors for the last time. 'Just moved out of the hotel. Weird as I've been there for 3 months!!! Had an emotional hug with the boys and we all teared up :(Josh, xx' he tweeted.

Meanwhile, excitement was building for the *X Factor* Final weekend. Although the pressure was off for Union J, like all the other finalists, they were heading up to Manchester, where the Final would be held for the first time ever, in front of a live audience of 10,000. There was a huge party atmosphere as the finalists joined forces onstage to perform a 'Hits of the Year' medley. Without any worries about performing to save their skins, Union J grinned happily as they entered – on scooters! – singing 'Payphone' by Maroon 5, followed by Kye Sones and District 3. ('Loved loved that group performance tonight. Not going to lie I was soooooo worried about falling on my face on that scooter lol! Josh, xx' Josh later tweeted.) Even Lucy Spraggan, who'd left the competition following illness, was back onstage and the atmosphere was electric.

For Christopher Maloney, Jahmene Douglas and James Arthur, this was the biggest night of their lives so far, and they gave it everything they had. Jahmene let his wilder side out with a dynamic performance of Curtis Mayfield's 'Move On Up' – Nicole was especially delighted to see the normally reticent singer let loose and dance a bit more on stage. Jahmene was enjoying himself, too, even cracking a joke that he'd try some gymnastics next time! It demonstrated the newly found confidence he'd developed over the course of the show. Christopher sang 'What a Feeling' from the movie *Fame* (after which Louis offered him a compliment for being the public's choice), but he was soon eclipsed by James Arthur taking on the blues classic 'Feeling Good'. Strolling on casually from backstage and performing a relatively stripped-back version of the song, his amazing voice was laid bare. All four judges rose to their feet in unison to applaud the modest singer. Tulisa's praise was again the loudest, anointing him the champion of the British music scene and someone the public should take to their hearts. Backstage, Union J were watching their friends and hoping that their favourite would win. 'Praying for Jahmene. Friend for life. He deserves it!!! Also BIG love to James too. Josh, x' wrote Josh.

Now there were only the mentor duets – which saw Nicole team up with both Jahmene and James, and Gary with Christopher – before the three finalists would become two. Jahmene and Nicole coped with near-disaster when one of their microphones stopped working, but could Jaymi and the other Union J boys' prediction that Christopher would win hold water? Nope – it appeared Jaymi's crystal ball had failed him, as Dermot O'Leary (in a super-swish tuxedo) announced that the acts through to Sunday night were Jahmene and James. Huge cheers burst forth from the crowd – and the judges – as Christopher was finally knocked out of the competition. Fears that a 'karaoke act' could win the biggest singing contest in the UK had been allayed. Either super-talented James or Jahmene would take the winner's crown.

Sunday saw time to celebrate for all the *X Factor* contestants. It was the last day of the competition and everyone was thrilled to see such big stars getting ready to perform along-side the finalists. Rihanna, Emeli Sandé and One Direction were all appearing, and for Union J in particular it was great to see their boyband brothers return to the *X Factor* stage. Seeing how far one band had come in just two years gave them hope for their future success. 'Watching One Direction rehearse. Wicked new song. Praying to be on that stage next year as a guest on xfactor! #Dreaming … Josh, x' tweeted Josh. But as the finalists gathered to perform their last ever group number, controversy struck again, as some of the contestants were missing. MK1, Lucy Spraggan and – incredibly – Christopher weren't there to sing a Christmas medley with the others. The reasons why soon transpired: MK1 were booked to appear at another venue, while Lucy Spraggan was due to duet on The Pogues' classic 'Fairytale of New York' with James Arthur but their segment had been cut from the final run-through. But what had happened to Christopher?

The next day's newspapers were filled with dramatic reports to explain why the third-placed singer hadn't shown. 'Christopher, 34, arrived for the run-through of the group song "clearly drunk", according to sources,' reported the *Sun*. 'After initially refusing to speak, he hit the roof after realising he only had one line in the medley. The sozzled Scouser – who was Gary Barlow's wild card and had made the final three – stormed back to his hotel. He failed to turn up at 11am for the second rehearsal – and eventually shipped up after noon, drunk.' The newspapers also claimed he had verbally abused fellow finalist Carolynne Poole and later begged to be asked back onto the show, but was refused. *The X Factor* would only release an official statement that read: 'Chris decided he no longer wanted to be part of *The X Factor* Final and has gone back to Liverpool.' It was a sad end to his involvement with the show.

Despite these absences, the other finalists gave the festive mash-up their all, with Union J the shining stars of the performance, enjoying this last moment performing to the nation as part of the *X Factor* family. Almost 12 million viewers, tuned in for Sunday's final show, and the boys knew they would never have another night like it. Still, the focus was on Jahmene and James as they battled it out, firstly picking their favourite songs that they'd sung earlier in the series. Jahmene performed a stunning version of Robbie Williams's 'Angels', while James brought back the incredible rendition of Marvin Gaye's 'Let's Get It On' that got him noticed in Week Eight. They then showcased their 'winner's singles' to the nation, with Jahmene covering the Beatles' classic 'Let It Be' and James singing 'Impossible', originally recorded by Barbadian singer Shontelle. Both delivered extraordinary, moving songs, their voices so different but each so impressive. Josh was bowled over watching his friends perform. 'Powerful incredible performance James Arthur. 2 worthy winners. Shame we couldn't of been there in the Final with them!!! Josh, x' he tweeted. It was clear that both deserved the *X Factor* crown, but who would take the winner's glory?

Union J waited nervously backstage with the other contestants to hear the final results. Who would be the winner of *The X Factor 2012*? The tension and excitement were at white heat. This was the culmination of all those weeks and months of hard graft, heartbreak and adrenalin. Millions of viewers were poised on the edge of their sofas and the noise in Manchester Central was deafening. Dermot announced the verdict to wild applause and screams – it was James! James looked utterly shocked as he hugged Jahmene and then his mentor, Nicole. It seemed almost too much for him to take in as he got to grips with the enormity of what had just happened.

With this declaration, *The X Factor* was nearly over for the year. But firstly, James had to perform his winner's song, 'Impossible'. As the song – and the series – reached its incredible climax, Union J ran onto the stage along with the other contestants and pulled their friend into a huge embrace. Ticker tape rained down onto the stage as everyone celebrated the end of an astonishing series. It had changed everyone's lives forever – including Union J's.

Christmas was now around the corner, and Union J couldn't wait for some time off to take stock of their amazing few months and relax with their families, who they'd barely seen in recent weeks. But they also had some big parties to contend with – firstly, the aftershow party at the Radisson hotel in Manchester on the Sunday night. George finally got the chance to chat to Little Mix – with whom he'd long wanted to duet – and the other boys rubbed shoulders with celebrities including David Hasselhoff and Michelle Keegan. They all had a brilliant time, with George snapped late into the night giving runner-up Jahmene a piggyback! Tuesday night saw Union J back in London for the series wrap party, held at London's Hippodrome Casino in the West End. Yet again, Christopher was a notable absentee as he tweeted he was 'too unwell' to celebrate with the other contestants. But Union J had a blast, enjoying the champagne and Jäger bombs that were flowing freely. As they said goodbye to their fellow *X Factor* contestants – at least until the upcoming tour in 2013 – the band were feeling emotional. 'I love you Jahmene with all my heart bro!!! Josh, x' tweeted Josh. Good news followed, as James Arthur's single became the fastest-selling winner's single so far, reaching 490,000 downloads in its first week of sales. It was a deserving Number One hit for the singer, who'd battled through some difficult times to make it.

The next two weeks saw Union J adjust to life after *The X Factor*, but although the boys were out of the TV series bubble, it was hardly a return to their previous lives. They immediately embarked on a mini-tour around the country to connect with the fans who had followed them over the past few months. The following Saturday saw them perform a gig at Cardiff's Pulse nightclub, one of the best-known gay clubs in the UK. Performing Carly Rae Jepsen's 'Call Me Maybe', they had a blast and reached out to their growing gay fanbase. 'Thank you Cardiff!!!! Hope you enjoyed your-selves as much as we did!! Josh and George, xx' the boys tweeted after their late-night gig. They were working hard again that week, gigging all around the country and showing their loyal *X Factor* fans that they were not going to disappear now that the show was over. Meanwhile, it was heads-down time as the boys and their manager, Blair Dreelan, worked hard to secure Union J the best record deal possible. They had come off *The X Factor* on a huge high, proving they had a huge fanbase, and the possibility of becoming – as Louis might say – the next big boyband. Serious business heads were needed, so Union J began building a team around them. Reports swirled that the boys were being offered a few different deals, and they leant on mentor Louis during this time to help them through the overwhelming process. 'Louis always looks after his acts and he knows exactly what they need to do,' reported the *Sun*. 'They've already had massive interest from labels and a few offers.' Finally, Union J decided on the deal to strike – with Sony Records, also home to their fellow contestants Ella Henderson and James Arthur.

They chose a familiar environment to break the good news on the Monday morning before Christmas: *Daybreak*. After appearing on the show many times during *The X Factor*, they were now coming in off their own backs. Dressed in cute retro-style Christmas sweaters, the boys broke out of the festive 'Sexy Snowman' set with smiles on their faces. 'Congratulations – you now have a record deal!' said presenter Aled Jones, and the boys looked thrilled. 'It's been a crazy week,' admitted Jaymi. 'Obviously our dream was to get a record deal and now we're going to Sony later on to sign contracts. So hopefully before Christmas we will have our deal finalised!' The boys looked happy and relaxed as they talked about being able to get together with their families after so many months apart. 'It's been nice to have some family time and catch up on real life,' said George. 'But it's weird: we've been in this bubble for three months, then we go home and there's Christmas trees everywhere! We're like, when did it become Christmas?' And despite now not seeing their *X Factor* pals every day, it wouldn't be long before the tour kicked off in the New Year. 'We're not going to be apart for that much longer,' grinned Josh. 'We're looking forward to the reunion – it should be good.' 'It's going to be a messy bus!' laughed Jaymi.

It was Christmas time and finally an opportunity for the boys to rest. As they headed back to their families, so much had changed – not least the fact that they were now tweeting their every move to hundreds of thousands of fans. 'HAHA my little brothers Leo and Archie say hi!' George wrote, attaching a cute photo of his siblings. 'First sleepover with my little brother for ages!!! Missed him alot :D Josh, x' wrote Josh on Christmas Eve. Even on Christmas Day, the boys decided to start a #UnionJFollowSpreeChristmasDay hashtag, only stopping for a break when their Christmas dinners were ready! It caused a Twitter sensation, trending worldwide. Each penned a personal message for the fans, too: 'Merry Christmas everybody. Love you all. Jaymi, x'; 'Merry Christmas :D :D Father Christmas spoilt me!!!!! Josh, x'; 'Merry Christmas everyone! What did you all get? Love George' and 'Want to say massive merry xmas to all of you. Hope you got everything you want. Thanks so much for all your support, love you all. JJ, x' It was certainly the happiest Christmas yet for Union J. As they tucked into feasts with their loved ones, they could wave goodbye to an incredible 2012 and welcome in an even more exciting 2013.

CHAPTER 14

NEW YEAR, NEW FUTURE: 2013 AND BEYOND

'HAPPY NEW YEAR EVERYONE :D thank u SO much for all your incredible support you have given Union J in 2012. Now let's make 2013 INSANE! Josh, x' tweeted Union J in the first few minutes of the New Year. The future certainly looked bright as the boys regrouped to begin work on making Union J a success. Josh returned from a short break in Paris and then the boys were ready to start gigging around the country again, as they'd been doing ever since leaving *The X Factor* in December 2012. But almost straight away disaster struck, as George had an accident on 2 January. 'So sorry to everyone in Ireland. I have had an accident so we won't be able to perform tomorrow so our gigs have been pulled. Sorry, George,' he tweeted. Fans flooded Twitter with messages of sympathy and the gossip speculated wildly that George was in hospital, had been burned or had received a life-threatening injury. The Union J team didn't confirm what exactly had happened to him, although eventually their tour manager, Mark Sutton, took to his own Twitter page to put the fans' minds at rest. 'OK, let's put this to sleep. I can tell you George had to attend hospital after receiving a nasty injury. His [sic] not dead or dying as speculated. He will be 100% fine in a few days. He sends his love and thanks to all concerned,' he wrote.

It was a dramatic – and unexpected – start to the New Year, but soon enough George was fully recovered and back with the band. JJ even managed to sneak in a few days' break with his family at Disneyland Paris. He'd had such a great time there with the *X Factor* crew in November 2012 that he made a proper trip of it, posting cute pics on Twitter showing all of the Hamblett clan wearing Mickey and Minnie Mouse ears. Over the course of the last few months, Union J had been asked what their one wish for 2013 would be. 'That we get to Number One,' George told *ITN News* back in December. 'Oh my God, that would be incredible!' gasped Jaymi. 'How amazing would it be to listen to *The Chart Show* on Sunday night and hear yourself in the chart?' mused Josh. Now out of the *X Factor* TV show bubble, it was time to turn those pipe dreams into a reality. The boys now had to decide what sort of band they were going to be, and what sort of songs they would put out. 'When we get out of the show we really want to go away, find out who we are as artists and then come out with our own sound and our own style,' Jaymi told ThisIsMax.net in November.

The last few months had meant so much to them, and now Jaymi was ready to create a permanent reminder of his life-changing time on *The X Factor*. Just a few days into 2013, he visited a tattoo parlour to get a huge new inking on his right arm. It depicted a microphone around which swirled musical symbols – a treble clef and notes on a stave, as well as a Union Jack. Jaymi was thrilled with his new personalised artwork. 'YEAH BUDDDDY!!! My new tattoo @

adrenalintattoo #lovingit #unionjtattoos,' he tweeted. It was obvious what most of the symbols represented – music, *The X Factor* and Union J – but fans were puzzled as to what the '24' in the middle meant. One keen-eyed JCat tweeted Jaymi's boyfriend Olly Marmon to find out what it was all about. '@emilywalker007 the 24 is our anniversary, both our birthdays, and he was born in the 2nd month and I'm the 4th month 🔱 x' Olly explained to a chorus of 'awwws'. Tattoo addict Jaymi now had 20 inkings on his body, and he wasn't finished yet.

In lots of ways, life in the first few weeks of 2013 felt much like being on *The X Factor* – apart from the absence of live television shows each weekend! The boys spent their time ferociously gigging around the country and rehearsing with their fellow contestants for the upcoming *X Factor* 2013 Live Tour. Just as before, each day girls congregated outside the London rehearsal studios to meet Union J, give them hugs and get autographs. It was fantastic for the band to be reunited with their *X Factor* family and they spent their days mixing hard work honing their numbers with laughter and messing about during breaks. The boys couldn't wait to start performing to huge arena crowds – sometimes in the same location where they had auditioned for *The X Factor* the previous year. 'It will be weird to go back and perform as a four-piece because we auditioned as Triple J and George was a solo singer,' Jaymi told *Teen Now* magazine. And the boys were really enjoying connecting with fans on their own series of smaller gigs around the country – although they were somewhat taken aback by the sorts of presents thrown at them by fans. 'One girl threw a bracelet at me onstage so

I put it on, and then I had a bra thrown at me – I didn't put that on, though,' said Josh. 'It's a shame our female fans throw their underwear at us because it would be much handier if they threw new men's pants – I could always do with some new underwear!' joked Jaymi.

Union J's friend Rylan Clark was in the *Celebrity Big Brother* house during this time, although it was revealed by his fellow housemate, former *EastEnders'* actress Gillian Taylforth, that he was actually popping out to attend the *X Factor* tour rehearsals! While this revelation caused online controversy, it didn't prevent the popular star from winning the competition outright, just a couple of days before the *X Factor* tour began. Union J were right behind their friend as he triumphed on reality TV. 'So proud of you @rylanclark. Really really deserve it. Cant wait to see you in a few hours!!!! Missed ya!!' tweeted Josh.

In between gigs and rehearsals for the live tour, Union J busied themselves with laying the groundwork for their new life as a proper boyband. It was finally confirmed in January 2013 that their record deal with RCA records, a division of Sony, was signed, sealed and delivered. This meant they shared a label with superstars such as Justin Timberlake, Britney Spears and Beyoncé, as well as successful fellow *X Factor* alumni Alexandra Burke and JLS. Union J were honoured to be in such incredible company and knew this boded well for their future. George even sweetly tweeted, 'Get butterflies when I see "Union J" on the RCA website.'

Ahead of the *X Factor* tour, the boys made another appearance on *Daybreak*, where they were now on really friendly terms with host Lorraine Kelly. She asked them directly about rumours in the press that claimed the boys had 'dumped' Louis Walsh and didn't want him involved in their burgeoning career. 'We love Louis, and Louis was incredible for us during the show. We've met loads of managers, including Oritsé from JLS,' revealed Josh – the JLS singer had recently set up his own pop management company. Jaymi was upfront and honest about the process the boys were going through and how they'd come to make up their minds about who would be in Team Union J. 'When we came out of *The X Factor* and were looking for new management, it was really important that we made the right decision,' he explained. 'So we met with lots of people, weighed up the pros and cons and we have made a decision and we're extremely happy with it.'

The boys had signed with Crown Talent Group, who also managed the careers of Jessie J and Sugababes. Any disappointment that the group hadn't won *The X Factor* were long gone, and the knowledge that JLS and One Direction had started their pop careers much as Union J were doing now gave them a real boost. 'It gives you that little bit of hope to know you actually don't need to win to have a great career outside,' said JJ. 'It's a great platform to have and cross fingers we'll have a good career.' 'At the time we were gutted not to make the Final, but looking back at it now, we were so happy with how well we did,' added Josh. 'And hopefully we've got enough exposure now to release a single and hopefully people will buy into it.'

Excitingly, just as Josh said, that month the boys headed into the studio to record their debut single – which was as yet shrouded in mystery. 'Recording our first single on

Monday! So sorry Belfast but we have to change the gig date, things are moving so fast for us! We'll be back! X' they tweeted giddily. 'It's what we've wanted to do for years and years, and hopefully we'll record an amazing song,' Josh told *Daybreak*. Set for a release date in June 2013, fans were desperate to hear what the boys had laid down, but it would be a long wait. It didn't stop the boys from sending teaser tweets out to their avid followers, though: 'Love love love how our first single is sounding already!!!! Excited lol. Josh x'

It had been obvious throughout the whole *X Factor* process, but Union J were using Twitter more than ever to communicate with their fans. Every day saw tweets from all four members – although more often than not it was Josh and George chatting to fans, telling them what they were up to, asking what they wanted to hear from the band and starting Union J hashtags. Even Jaymi's mum Jackie had joined the social networking site and chatted daily with her son's fans. JCats felt hugely connected to their favourite group, and the number of followers of UnionJWorld was growing incredibly quickly. By mid-January, they celebrated reaching 800,000 followers (after starting a hashtag to reach the milestone, naturally) – which was pretty impressive for a band yet to release their first single. By spring 2013 they had more than 900,000 fans, meaning the magic million wouldn't be far off.

The long-awaited *X Factor* 2013 Live Tour kicked off in Manchester on 26 January – the city which only a few weeks before had hosted the Final of the *X Factor* series. Arriving at Manchester Piccadilly station in the city centre, the acts found they were now fully fledged celebrities, with lots of fans out there. Crowds gathered to meet their idols as excitement about seeing their *X Factor* favourites onstage grew. For hundreds of thousands of fans across the country, this would be the first time they were able to actually see them in the flesh rather than on TV. And for Union J, the thrill of performing to such huge crowds each night was beyond exciting. Naturally they were nervous, but after months of preparation and practice on *The X Factor* TV show, as well as doing their own smaller gigs, they felt ready as a group. 'Cant believe our 1st date on the tour is tonight in Manchester!! It only feels like yesterday that we were auditioning for the show!! Josh x' tweeted Josh, just hours before they took to the stage.

The show was a triumph: Rylan Clark kicked off proceedings with his flamboyant version of 'Gangnam Style' and revisited his Spice Girls medley, which had won everyone over in Week Six of the live shows. Ella Henderson showcased her glam side in a sparkly top and skirt as she sung Cher's 'Believe', while James Arthur brought the house down with his Number One single 'Impossible'. But, of course, Union J were the main attraction for thousands of cheering JCats. They performed their favourite songs from the series: Taylor Swift's 'Love Story', 'Call Me Maybe' by Carly Rae Jepsen and the amazing mash-up of 'Bleeding Love' and 'Broken Strings' that had earned them such a fantastic reception in Week Two. The first nights in Manchester went down a storm, with *X Factor* fans having the time of their lives. And they were not alone – it was an incredible moment for Union J, too. 'Best 2 days EVER! Amazing fun touring in Manchester, so loud! :P Cant wait for Tuesday now :D Thanks for all our banners! George X,' tweeted George. 'Wow, today the crowd was even better. The support in Manchester is amazing and great to perform up here!! Thanks for the support!! JJ x' JJ wrote.

Despite the controversy around his involvement in the *X Factor* tour (and a brief movement to have him replaced by Kye Sones), Christopher Maloney soon settled into touring life with his fellow *X Factor* contestants. He and Jaymi even took a break while on the Liverpool stretch of the tour to get new tattoos done together. Christopher opted for a combination of a rose, some lyrics and the date of his *X Factor* audition, while Jaymi went for some lines of script on the inside of his left arm. It was clear from their friendly banter that there were no hard feelings between them, and all the negative publicity around Christopher and *The X Factor* series appeared to have been forgotten.

Life on tour was full of fun. For the 26 dates, the *X Factor* 'Final Seven' travelled the length and breadth of the UK and Ireland – from Liverpool to Glasgow, Dublin to Birmingham, London to Cardiff and beyond. The boys shouted out every day on Twitter to the local crowds coming to see them and constantly tweeted snaps of themselves enjoying their down-time, which often involved eating, watching scary films and playing Xbox. In spare moments, George attempted to teach his bandmate Jaymi how to play guitar. And JJ showed off his raunchy side by posing for a sexy photo with none other than Rylan! The two friends posted a cheeky snap of JJ pretending to take a bite out of Rylan's neck, with the caption reading: 'Sorry girls. Me and JJ @unionjworld have something to tell you.' And clever Rylan was having an incredible 2013. Not only had he won *Celebrity Big Brother*, he was also making money from personal appearances, merchandise and a record deal. *Now* magazine estimated he would make £2 million before the end of the year.

Jaymi had earlier predicted that one of the breakout stars of *The X Factor* would indeed be his Essex mate, forecasting that he would not only have a terrific TV career but also have a big cheesy pop hit, similar to Psy's global dance craze 'Gangnam Style'. Mystic Jaymi might not have got his prediction right about Christopher winning *The X Factor*, but it looked as if he was on the nose with Rylan.

A few days before the end of the *X Factor* tour, Jaymi celebrated his twenty-third birthday in fabulous Jaymi style. He was joined by his mum Jackie, boyfriend Olly and little brother Aaron, and they all dressed up in onesies (the birthday boy wearing his now-legendary black-and-white number) and posed with glasses of champagne before posting the snap on Twitter. It had been an amazing birthday for Jaymi – performing at Wembley Arena before being joined by his nearest and dearest and trending on the social media site as well. The final night of the tour – 28 February 2013, in Belfast – saw Union J decide to go out in style … literally. The boys dressed up in Ella Henderson's clothes – and bizarrely Josh actually suited the sparkly gold-and-blue top. 'This is how we dressed for the final song on tour tonight!!! Hahahaha!!! Yes, Josh is wearing Ella's outfit! Heels and all! G x' wrote George.

Finishing the tour marked the real end of the *X Factor* journey for Union J. No longer would they be part of the *X Factor* brand, either through the live shows or as part of a group tour. Soon the producers would be auditioning a new round of wannabes, who were applying in droves for *The X Factor 2013*. Now it was time for Union J to strike out on their own for good and try to make a success of themselves as an independent boyband. They kept busy in the next few months, teaming up with other celebrities to support Red Nose Day and raising money for charities in Africa and the UK on 15 March 2013. As a Comic Relief stunt, the boys bravely took on the 'Cinnamon Challenge' on Nick Grimshaw's Radio 1 breakfast show. With celebrities such as Little Mix, Conor Maynard and even supermodel Kate Moss watching, George attempted to eat a whole teaspoon of the spice, but spat it out and had to run to the toilets to stop himself from being sick! At Radio 1, they met up with Jessie J, who would famously shave her head on the live show later that day. Hitting it off with the feisty star, Union J soon announced they'd be appearing at her AllStarz Summer Party in June. Already they had set up some big summer gigs in Chester, Alton Towers, London, Pontypridd and Reading, among many others, to tie in with the new single – it was to be a busy summer for the boys. In the few months between the tour and Union J's single release, they were working hard behind the scenes, but kept their fans in the loop as much as possible. Everyone was desperately keen to find out more about what the boys were working on, but they would have to be patient. 'We will always be the same Union J and love you all as always :) Everything has been a bit crazy lately but you will love whats coming up! X' they tweeted in March.

The bitterly cold spring of 2013 also marked a special anniversary for Union J. It seemed unbelievable, but it had only been a year since they first travelled to their *X Factor* auditions, the initial step on a journey that had led to unimagined fame and excitement. On 25 March, George looked back to the same date, 12 months before: 'A year ago today I was getting on that train to go to my very first x factor audition!! What a year!!! George X' He couldn't have put it any better. Not even the most ambitious *X Factor* auditionee could imagine the life-changing moments that had happened to the four ordinary members of Union J.

The boys spent the next few months working hard. Although the weekly ritual of *The X Factor* was a distant memory by now, and some TV viewers might have wondered where the Union J boys had got to, the fans knew otherwise. Communicating daily with their followers via Twitter, the boys kept them informed of the rounds of recording, the photoshoots and tour preparations that were ongoing, laying the groundwork for their big summer and beyond. Not only would they be appearing at lots of summer festivals, but Josh revealed an even bigger surprise: 'OHHHH AND JUST TO LET EVERYONE KNOW we are doing a Union J big tour at the end of the year :) :) :) :) Josh x' For thousands of JCats, the time couldn't pass quickly enough.

What's more, there were huge changes in their personal lives, too. After a couple of days relaxing at Champneys spa hotel in Hertfordshire, Jaymi and his boyfriend Olly decided to make a big lifestyle decision. They were moving house – and would move in with JJ! The boys found a 'beautiful' apartment in London and after moving in during the month of March, they had the rest of the Union J gang over for a housewarming. With George and Josh getting their own places in London, too, it was the first time they'd all lived in the capital city and it was a thrill for everyone – especially the more obsessed fans who soon found where they were living, much to the boys' amazement. 'The girls have built up somehow, I'm not too sure how. There's always girls outside,' George told *Metro*. 'We thought everyone was going to forget us, normally there's a calm before the storm after *X Factor* before you release a single.'

Since the Ella Henderson rumours had finally died down, with Ella confirming that she was focusing on her career rather than a relationship, the three single boys of Union J – George, Josh and JJ – hadn't been linked with anyone else. They even claimed that they were terrible at approaching girls! 'To be honest with you, we are quite bad with chat-up lines. We are like four geeks,' added George. 'We're all single.' Something for which their hundreds of thousands of fans were very thankful.

By the beginning of April 2013, it was finally time for the big reveal. After months of speculation, Union J were ready to officially announce the name of their first ever single, which would be out on 2 June. For days, Twitter was abuzz, with fans excitedly sharing their anticipation, and the hashtag #unionjsingletitle trended worldwide. And it wasn't just the fans chomping at the bit to get the news out there. 'So who is looking forward to the single name tonight??? Buzzing to tell all of you woop, JJ x,' Jamie wrote. By 7pm on the evening of 8 April, the news was out. Counting down on a specially recorded livestream video, the boys yelled in unison, 'It's called "CARRY YOU!"' Urging the fans to show their love and support through buying the record when it came out on 2 June, George was amazed by the thought that it would be played on the radio in the next few weeks. 'That's going to be the weirdest thing ever!' he grinned. 'Our first single coming out!' The boys were brimming with excitement as they joked about starting a new hashtag for the single. 'We carry you, so what do you carry?' asked Jaymi. 'I carry my Tesco carrier bag,' deadpanned Josh.

Fans were of course dying to hear what the song sounded like, but there would be another two weeks before it played on the radio. Meanwhile, the Union J boys did their best to give them a taster. 'It's a great pop song and we're excited to be performing it. It's very catchy,' explained Jaymi. Website Popjustice.com agreed, giving it the seal of approval: 'We love it. It is a proper big, honest and direct boyband pop single.' Written by pop supremo Steve Mac – who'd also penned hits for the likes of Westlife, One Direction, The Wanted and JLS, as well as George's favourite Little Mix song, 'Turn Your Face' – the single was also praised for managing to create a Union J 'sound', something the boys were really pleased about. 'It's about being there for each other. It symbolises us as a band – that we're here for each other,' Jaymi told the site. 'It makes me think of driving along, being at a red light, and the car next to us having the window down and the song blaring,' added Josh. 'It's quite a summer tune – well, that's the plan!' As well as filming the video for their first single ('It's cool actually, we've just seen the first edit and we're so hyped. It's not going to be what people are expecting from a boyband off the back of *The X Factor*. It's completely different, so we just hope the public buy into it,' said Jaymi, tantalisingly), the band also revealed their swishy new logo – a simple joined-up script reading 'Union J', with a flourish underneath. The 'Carry You' cover artwork created a huge stir, showing the boys looking gorgeous and Jaymi debuting a new, more sideswept hairstyle. The next few weeks were spent finishing up the album in the studio and announcing more and more summer gigs.

Things really hotted up once 'Carry You' was unleashed upon the airwaves. The boys had lined up two appearances in the early hours of Monday 22 April at 7:45am on Capital Radio and 8:15am on Radio 1. The night before their big day, anticipation was at fever pitch and George took to Twitter to share his feelings with fans. 'Feeling emotional. We love you all so much. Single being played tmrw and we wouldn't be anywhere without you, every last one of you! <3 G x' he wrote. After only a few hours' sleep, the band rocked up in the Capital FM studios to meet presenters Lisa Snowdon and Dave Berry. It was time to play the single for the first time.

'What kind of sound have you gone for then, boys?' asked Lisa. 'It's quite different to what people were maybe expecting from us,' explained Jaymi. 'But it's true to us. It's a feel-good, upbeat summer song.' The moment had arrived as the song began. Simple, strong piano chords introduced the first few bars and George's voice rang out. As Jaymi took over lead vocals a pumping dance beat was added, and soon all four boys were singing the chorus together – a hugely catchy repetition of the title, complete with an everyone-join-in 'Carry you-oo!' refrain. It was everything the fans could have wished for – a brilliantly crafted slice of pop genius that would have everyone humming and singing along that summer.

As the track faded out, Dave Berry asked the boys how it felt to finally hear their song on the radio. The build-up had been a long time coming. 'It's really surreal,' admitted JJ. 'We've wanted this for all of our lives.' 'I didn't ever think in my life I would be on the radio,' added George. 'We've worked so hard the last seven months and it's all come down to this,' said an earnest Josh. 'Today's the day we've wanted for our whole lives and it's a dream come true.'

Starting the hashtag #1sttimeiheardcarryyoustory, Union J could see straight away how much their fans had taken to the song. 'I cried uncontrollably. I am so proud of my 4 boys. Forever a JCAT. I've even got the lyrics learnt off already!' tweeted one, reflecting the reaction of thousands. Even girl group The Saturdays added in their compliments, writing, 'LOVING your new single guys, been in our heads all day!'

As thousands rushed to pre-order the song on iTunes, the band took stock of what had been a crucial day for Union J: they had finally showed the world what they were made of. And what a reaction – it had been better than the band could have dreamed of. 'Today has been a special day :D thanku to EVERY single one of you for believing in us and for show-ing all your "Carry You" Support! Josh xx' wrote Josh on Twitter that night. The good feeling carried on into the next day as the single raced up the iTunes pre-order chart. 'I am such a lucky lad to be in a band with the 3 most incredible lads in the world ... JJ, Jaymi and George!! Love you boys :D <3 josh xxx' wrote Josh.

Just one short week later, fans were in for yet another treat as the boys released their video online. On their website, the band posted a smart-looking 'invite' for fans to watch the video premiere, on Monday, 29 April at 4.45pm precisely. Counting down the minutes on Twitter, Union J were clearly as excited as their fans were. 'LETS GET THIS NO.1 TRENDING #unionjlivestream!!' the band tweeted giddily. They began the evening by answering Twitter questions from fans on the livestream. Pulling daft faces and demonstrating the brotherly banter the fans now knew so well, the boys revealed that their second single was likely to be out in September, and that Josh would shave his head for charity! As the big reveal grew closer, it was clear the band desperately wanted to hear the genuine reaction, with Jaymi urging, 'Tell us what you love about it, your favourite bits, we're really interested to find out what you guys think of it.' 'You need to show it to each of your friends at least 30,000 times,' deadpanned Josh. George quickly retorted with, 'I think that's a *little* OTT ...' As the band built up to the moment of truth, Josh cheekily wiggled his backside to the cameras and the boys yelled out in excitement. It was time!

The first few seconds of the video saw Union J's new logo scrawl across the screen as the boys queued up outside the Maze club in Nottingham Then the already familiar piano chords and electric tones of 'Carry You' begin, showing the bandmates getting ready to perform a gig in front of fans. The video certainly gave JCats what they wanted. It featured lots of stunning footage of the boys: George in a café staring moodily at the camera, JJ messing around on a bike, Josh getting a haircut and Jaymi browsing in a vinyl record store. It felt intimate and personal, which was how the fans related to their heroes after going on such a dramatic journey with them over the past few months. And it showcased the boys as a new band of ordinary young guys – in the video, they perform at an 'open mic' night in front of a small crowd – who were speaking to their fans directly with their promise to 'Carry You'. It was a perfect example of the video capturing how they were in real life. Still on the verge of superstardom, it was symbolic of where they'd come from and hopeful for their future success.

The fans immediately shouted out their approval as the video was posted on the band's official Vevo YouTube site. 'This song … love it … amazing,' wrote one, while another posted, 'Really like this, so catchy. They all have amazing voices.' Capital FM posted screengrabs from the video to sate public appetite for as much of the boys as it could get. It was an amazing time for fans of the band, as almost every day there was new Union J news and visuals. Just a few days later George unveiled the official JCats logo. In the same font as the Union J logo, it gave fans their own identity. And within a few days, the boys knew just how much the fans loved their video as it reached an amazing one million views online in only a week.

With the next few weeks crucial to the single's success, the publicity machine for Union J kicked into overdrive. The boys gave interviews to various publications, including the *Sun* newspaper, in which George promised to 'sit in a bath of beans' if they reached number one. And Jaymi revealed that JJ's domestic habits left a lot to be desired. 'JJ hasn't found the iron, the hoover or the washing machine yet. He doesn't know how to use any of them,' he sighed. 'And when he goes to the toilet and the loo roll runs out, rather than replacing it, he'll just go to a different toilet. Very lazy, JJ!' The band appeared on the cover of *Top of the Pops* magazine, gave interviews to *Star* and *Bliss* magazines, and even had a cheeky 'virtual date' chat with *Heat* magazine. They embarked on a radio station tour across the UK, packing in visits to Glasgow, Edinburgh and Newcastle in just one day. The boys also performed a storming gig at Future Hits Live in Newcastle and even presented a gong at the British Soap Awards on ITV1. To screams from the celeb-packed crowd, the band presented the Sexiest Female award to Michelle Keegan, who plays Tina McIntyre in ITV's *Coronation Street* – who joked, 'My night's made!' as she got to give each of the boys a kiss.

It was unrelenting, the craziest few weeks of Union J's career so far as they pulled out all the stops to take their debut single as high up the charts as possible. But throughout it all, the boys were clearly having the time of their lives, enjoying the connection with their fans and constantly posting funny videos online. Their livestreams were hosted weekly, as was the band's new idea: Challenge Union J, where JCats sent in different ideas for the boys to follow.

The first saw the lads trying to 'expand their minds' by being put under hypnosis by mind-maestro Ben Dali. JJ and George soon found themselves in a deep trance and were convinced they were champion jockeys, winning the Grand National. 'I'd definitely do it again,' said a dazed JJ. The next challenge saw the bandmates undergo a lie-detector test to see who was the most honest. It was another hilarious undertaking, although the lie detector test thought Jaymi wasn't being honest when he said he was in Union J! They also regularly updated their websites with 'Secret Union', featuring hidden truths about the band, and posted online behind-the-scenes fun from the 'Carry You' video shoot in a freezing-cold Nottingham. 'This has been the best two days of our lives,' declared an emotional Jaymi to the cameras after the video shoot. 'We literally feel like proper pop stars now, it's amazing!'

Throughout all the fun and hard work, the boys knew the moment of truth was fast approaching and they were both nervous and thrilled about the upcoming single release. Time was marching on. 'Hang on ... So Carry You is out in 2 weeks?! WHAAAT! It's all happening so fast!! Who's excited? George X' tweeted George. And he had still more tweets to tease the fans with as he started the hashtag #unionjannouncement in late May, leading to fevered online speculation that the boys would finally confirm the dates of their first proper tour.

Finally, the day arrived: Sunday 9 June 2013. It was a doubly exciting day for the boys as they were also due to play the Capital FM Summertime Ball at Wembley Stadium, alongside such huge stars as Olly Murs, Robbie Williams, Taylor Swift and Jessie J. It was the culmination of so many years of dreaming for all four members of the group, and they couldn't have been happier as they performed 'Carry You' and their famous cover of 'Call Me Maybe' to a cheering crowd of thousands. It was the moment they realised that they were now bona fide pop stars. 'I have been in the audience of the Summertime Ball for the last five years,' Josh wrote on Twitter. 'To think I performed today is a dream. Thank you to everyone.'

They also received the news they'd been desperate to hear – 'Carry You' was a hit! They'd reached Number Six in the charts, which was a huge achievement against such tough competition as Daft Punk's summer smash 'Get Lucky'. They'd done it. Against the odds, and compared to a year ago when the band hadn't even existed, they now had a top-ten hit, over a million Twitter followers and thousands of devoted JCats. Josh added to his earlier Twitter message with more emotional, heartfelt words: 'Honestly I am the luckiest boy in the world. Today has been 1 of the best feelings ever. I am overwhelmed and so grateful for everything,' he wrote.

They were no longer four ordinary boys with a dream of making it; their dream had come true. Union J were set to take over the world.